teach ®
yourself

**computing for
the over 50s**

D0183283

teach yourself ®

computing for
the over 50s
bob reeves

Launched in 1938, the **teach yourself** series grew rapidly in response to the world's wartime needs. Loved and trusted by over 50 million readers, the series has continued to respond to society's changing interests and passions and now, 70 years on, includes over 500 titles, from Arabic and Beekeeping to Yoga and Zulu. What would you like to learn?

be where you want to be with **teach yourself**

For UK order enquiries: please contact Bookpoint Ltd, 130 Milton Park, Abingdon, Oxon OX14 4SB. Telephone: +44 (0) 1235 827720. Fax: +44 (0) 1235 400454. Lines are open 09.00–17.00, Monday to Saturday, with a 24-hour message answering service. Details about our titles and how to order are available at www.teachyourself.co.uk

For USA order enquiries: please contact McGraw-Hill Customer Services, PO Box 545, Blacklick, OH 43004-0545, USA. Telephone: 1-800-722-4726. Fax: 1-614-755-5645.

For Canada order enquiries: please contact McGraw-Hill Ryerson Ltd, 300 Water St, Whitby, Ontario L1N 9B6, Canada. Telephone: 905 430 5000. Fax: 905 430 5020.

Long renowned as the authoritative source for self-guided learning – with more than 50 million copies sold worldwide – the **teach yourself** series includes over 500 titles in the fields of languages, crafts, hobbies, business, computing and education.

British Library Cataloguing in Publication Data: a catalogue record for this title is available from the British Library.

Library of Congress Catalog Card Number: on file.

First published in UK 2006 by Hodder Education, part of Hachette Live UK, 338 Euston Road, London, NW1 3BH.

First published in US 2006 by The McGraw-Hill Companies, Inc.

The **teach yourself** name is a registered trade mark of Hodder Headline.

Typeset by Servis Filmsetting Ltd, Manchester.
Printed in Great Britain for Hodder Education, an Hachette Livre UK Company, 338 Euston Road, London NW1 3BH, by Cox & Wyman Ltd, Reading, Berkshire.

The publisher has used its best endeavours to ensure that the URLs for external websites referred to in this book are correct and active at the time of going to press. However, the publisher and the author have no responsibility for the websites and can make no guarantee that a site will remain live or that the content will remain relevant, decent or appropriate.

Hachette Livre UK's policy is to use papers that are natural, renewable and recyclable products and made from wood grown in sustainable forests. The logging and manufacturing processes are expected to conform to the environmental regulations of the country of origin.

Impression number   10 9 8
Year   2010 2009 2008

contents

preface

This book is specifically designed for the more mature newcomer to computers. It covers a comprehensive range of typical computer uses and assumes that the reader has no prior knowledge of using a computer.

Jargon has been kept to a minimum and where it has been used, it is clearly highlighted and referenced by a full 'jargon-busting' glossary with all glossary terms **highlighted in bold type** in the text.

Throughout this book, when you need to click on something on the screen, it will be shown in the text in single speech marks. For example, if you need to click on a menu on the screen called Save, the instruction will read: Click 'Save'. When you need to press one of the keys on the keyboard, the name of that key be shown in capitals. For example, if you need to press the ENTER key, the instructions will read: Press ENTER.

It is recommended that you work through the chapters in order, although you can dip in and out. Some chapters are best read together. In particular:

- Chapters 1–5 cover all of the basics
- Chapters 6 and 7 cover word processing (typing documents)
- Chapters 8 and 9 cover email
- Chapters 10–16 cover the Internet
- Chapters 17 and 18 cover digital photography
- Chapters 19 and 20 cover how to create safe copies of your work
- Chapters 21–23 cover the creation of various publications using desktop publishing software (e.g. posters, leaflets, etc.)
- Chapters 24 and 25 cover the use of spreadsheets when working with numerical or financial information

- Chapter 26 covers the creation of a database
- Chapter 27 covers the presentation of a slideshow

The intention of the book is to build up an arsenal of skills using a range of different computer programs. You will soon discover that skills learned in one aspect of computing can be transferred to others. There are hints and tips throughout the chapters to help you on your way.

The book features examples from the most common programs being used at present including Microsoft® Word, PowerPoint®, Excel®, Access and Publisher. Several other programs are used, many of which are freely available from the Internet.

One of the problems with computers is that the programs are changing all the time. When changes are made, a new 'version' is brought out. Therefore, there are lots of different versions of the same programs available. The good news is that this does not fundamentally change the way in which the program works. However, it does mean that some of the screens might look a bit different. This book uses Windows® XP Home Edition and Microsoft® Office 2000.

Finally, when you first start, computers can be a bit scary. One mature evening-class student commented that the computer screen is so cluttered it looks like a flight deck on an aeroplane with little buttons and signs all over the place. However, the big difference is that if you go wrong on the computer, it doesn't matter. Your computer is virtually impossible to break – so don't be scared of it, just click away and see what happens. Have fun.

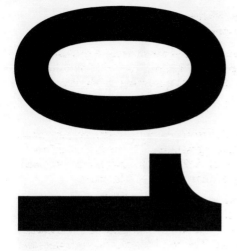

01

choosing a computer

In this chapter you will learn:

- what the main parts of the computer are
- how to understand a computer specification
- what specification of computer you need for the things you will be using your computer for
- whether to have a laptop or a desktop computer
- how to make your decision of what to buy and where to buy it

A screen, tower, keyboard and mouse © iStockphoto.com/Clément Contet

Aims of this chapter

There is a bewildering choice when it comes to buying a computer. There are hundreds of different options, and you can end up spending a lot of money on things that you don't really need. This chapter will help you to work out what computer will be the most suitable for the type of things for which you plan to use a computer. Whether you are buying a computer for the first time, or perhaps upgrading to a new one, this chapter will help you decide what to get.

1.1 What do you want to use your computer for?

You might not know the answer to this question yet! However, you may already know what you are *not* going to use your computer for and this might help you in your choice. The price of the computer is usually based on how fast it works and how much information you want to keep on it.

When you buy a computer the manufacturer will publish the specification of the computer. A basic **computer system** is made up of the base unit, sometimes called a tower, a screen, keyboard, mouse and printer. Computer equipment such as this is called **hardware**.

A printer © iStockphoto.com/Dennys Bisogno

You will also need what is called **software**. This refers to the programs that you will run on the computer. Programs are needed to let you do all the things you want to do like type letters, send emails and get onto the **Internet**.

1.2 What you will need

The base unit or tower is where all the clever stuff goes on. The main features to look for when you are choosing your computer are:

Processor

The processor is the brains of the computer. Everything that is done on the computer goes through the processor. The speed is measured in **gigahertz (GHz)**. The simple rule is the higher the number of GHz, the faster your computer will work. Anything over 2GHz is perfectly adequate for most computer users.

2.8GHz

Memory

This is sometimes called RAM (random access memory). This is measured in **megabytes (MB)**. The simple rule here is the higher the number of MB, the faster your computer will run. Anything over 256MB is perfectly adequate for most computer users although 512MB or more is recommended.

1024 MB

Hints and tips

How important is speed? All modern computers are fast. Most things you do on the computer such as typing documents, surfing the Internet, emailing, etc. do not require a really fast processor or lots of memory. If you plan to use your computer for playing computer games or editing movies, then faster processor speeds and more memory might be needed.

Hard disk (HDD)

This is the amount of information that the computer can store. This is measured in **gigabtyes (GB)** and, you guessed it – the bigger the number, the more information it will store. Anything over 40GB is more than adequate for most computer users.

80GB

CD or DVD drive

These are the trays on the front of the tower that slide out so that you can put in a CD or DVD. CDs and DVDs have all sorts of information on them including computer programs, data and films. It is recommended that you get a DVD drive as these will cope with CDs and DVDs. A CD drive will cope only with CDs. Sometimes the speed of the CD or DVD drive is shown. Anything over 52× is perfectly adequate for most computer users.

24×

> **Hints and tips**
> Computer manufacturers bring out new computers all of the time. They are always bringing out faster processors and increased memory. This means that your computer will start to become out of date quite quickly. This does not really matter for most users.

Monitor

This is the screen on which everything is displayed. As with the computer tower, there are thousands of variations to choose from. Most monitors now are flat, which means that they take up only a small amount of space on your desk. They also have less glare than the old-fashioned ones, so it is recommended to get a flat screen. The main decision is about the size of the screen. The size is measured in good old-fashioned inches. Standard sizes are from 15 to 19 inches. Bigger screens are more expensive but are much easier to read. The best advice is to go to a shop and have a look at the different sizes.

Keyboard and mouse

You don't usually get much choice with these as your computer will come with a standard keyboard and mouse. All keyboards are pretty much the same and you use them for typing in letters and numbers. The mouse is a pointing device. You point at things on the screen and click the buttons to make things happen. If you don't like wires everywhere, you can invest in a wireless mouse.

Hints and tips
Almost every keyboard is a QWERTY keyboard. This is due to the layout of the letters on the keyboard – the first six letters starting from the top left spell QWERTY. This layout is exactly the same as on typewriters.

Printer

This is for producing printed copies of anything you do on your computer. As with everything else to do with computers, there are thousands to choose from. The main decisions are whether you want an **inkjet** or a **laser** printer and whether you want colour or just black and white prints. Inkjets are cheaper to buy, but the ink cartridges can run out quickly and are expensive to replace. Laser printers are more expensive to buy, produce slightly better quality and print more quickly. Most computer users opt for an inkjet.

Colour printing is more expensive than black and white printing as you have to buy colour ink cartridges as well as black ones. However, unless the only thing you will be doing is typing documents, then a colour printer is going to be essential.

Hints and tips
Some printers can also be used as a **scanner** and a photocopier. If you think you will need to scan or copy documents, then it would be worth having a look at one of these.

1.3 The operating system (Windows® XP)

You will also need to choose what software you want. When you buy your hardware, you sometimes get some software with it. There is more on this in Chapter 3, but at this stage you must make sure that the computer you buy comes with an **operating system**.

This is a program that enables your computer to work and is essential. The most common operating system is Microsoft Windows®, which normally comes as part of the price of the computer. Make sure any computer you choose has this on it already.

> **Hints and tips**
> There are many different versions of Windows® and new versions come out all the time. Most new computers come with Windows® XP Pro or XP Home. Either of these is fine.

1.4 Plugging things in using USB ports

In the next chapter, you will learn about a range of additional **devices** that can be plugged into your computer. Most of these devices attach using a **USB** connection. Make sure your computer has got at least six **USB ports**. This will allow up to six different devices to be plugged in at the same time.

USB ports

1.5 Connecting to the Internet

If you want to connect to the Internet you will need a **modem**. This is a device that might be built into the computer, or may be plugged into the back. You have to choose which company to get your Internet connection from, for example Tiscali, BT, AOL, etc. and they will normally supply you with a modem to plug into one of the USB ports. The other end plugs into the telephone socket. If you have broadband, you will also be supplied with filters, which you need to plug into any other phone sockets. These enable you to make phone calls while using the Internet at the same time.

A modem

These days, you really should get **broadband** access, which is now available in most areas. Broadband means that the access to all of the information is quite quick. Without broadband, access is boringly slow.

1.6 Laptop or desktop?

The computers discussed so far relate to **desktop** computers. As the name suggests, these are computers that you keep in one place (on your desk) at home. In the examples before, you would put your tower unit on, or under your desk.

A laptop computer

Another option is to go portable and get a **laptop**. Laptops have all the same bits as a desktop, but they are all put together into one portable unit. The keyboard, mouse and screen are all part of the laptop contained within the casing. Laptops are light, portable and run for about four hours on batteries. You can plug them in and recharge them at home or even on trains these days.

You can do exactly the same thing with a laptop as with a desktop. So, should you get one? On the plus side, they are portable, take up less space in your house, can be used anywhere and do everything a desktop can do. On the downside, they are more expensive to buy, more easily lost or stolen and some people don't like the smaller keyboards and screens that they tend to have. Unless you have a really good reason to go for a laptop, it is recommended that you stick with a desktop.

1.7 Where to get your computer from

As you will discover when you try to buy a computer, there are several different manufacturers to choose from and you can buy from a range of places. Generally speaking, you get what you pay for and it pays to shop around.

High Street chains: These are quite competitive on price and have a good selection of computers. They are a safe bet if you don't have a good local specialist.

Specialist computer shops: The level of advice you get will probably be a lot better in a specialist computer shop, though they may not be able to be as competitive on price. They are usually good at looking after you if you have any problems later. It's good if you can find one that comes recommended.

The Internet/mail order: You can get some real bargains from catalogues and the Internet (if you have access). Internet and mail order businesses don't have the overheads that the shops do and this is how they can do it cheaper. The disadvantage is that you won't get to see the computer 'in the flesh' before you buy it. Use a bigger company that you have heard of or that has been recommended. You could always find the computer you want in a shop and then see if you can get the same thing cheaper on the Internet.

Warranties: Most new computers come with at least one year's warranty although this can be extended to three. Most warranties require the computer to be sent to the manufacturer, which means you will be without it for a week or so.

Summary

In this chapter we have discussed:
- What hardware (equipment) you need
- What 'specification' of computer you need
- Desktop and laptop computers
- Where to get a computer from

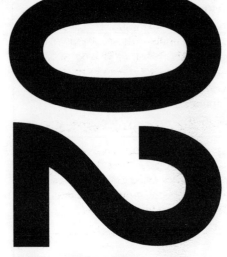

02

other equipment that you might need

In this chapter you will learn:

- what other computer equipment you might need
- what specification of equipment is needed

Aims of this chapter

Once you have chosen the basic computer system, you are now faced with another bewildering selection of equipment and devices that you can plug into your computer. These are sometimes referred to as computer **peripherals**. This chapter aims to explain the most common peripherals and advise on whether you need them or not, and what type to buy.

2.1 What peripherals do you need?

Many of the **peripherals** that you can buy have quite specific functions, so it is not worth investing in them unless you have good reason to do so. Most devices these days plug into your computer using a **USB** connection and your computer should have at least six **USB ports** for you to plug in to.

Hints and tips

Most devices are now 'plug and play', which means that when you plug them in, the computer spots that they have been plugged in and they will work automatically.

Digital camera

These are now more common than old-fashioned cameras. They do not use film. Instead, they store the image electronically on a **card** that slots into the camera. You can store hundreds of images on a card and can transfer the images onto your computer where you can store and print them.

The main things to look for when buying a digital camera are:

Mega pixels: This refers to the number of tiny dots used to make up the image. The larger the number of mega pixels, the better clarity you get in your finished photographs. Anything over 3 mega pixels is adequate for the average photographer.

Optical and digital zoom: This refers to the amount of magnification you can get, i.e. how far you can focus in on images that are far away. Optical zoom is better as it is achieved using the camera's lens; 3× optical zoom is usually sufficient. Digital zoom digitally zooms in on the image; 6× digital zoom is perfectly adequate.

LCD: This is the small screen that you use to **preview** the image. The size is measured in inches; 2.5 inches is adequate although larger screens are easier to see.

> **Hints and tips**
> You can also buy digital camcorders, which you can use to record moving images. Like a digital camera, you can transfer the images onto your computer where you can watch the film you have made.

Web cam

A web cam © iStockphoto.com/Mark Hayes

This is a camera that you place on top of your screen, which takes moving pictures of you! The idea of this is that you can contact people using your computer and they can see and hear you while you are talking to them. If they have a web cam at their end, you can see them too. These are particularly useful if you have friends in other countries that you would like to see and hear, rather than just write to. Choose one that has a **resolution** of 640×480 or higher. The higher the resolution, the clearer the images will be. If you want to be heard, you will need a web cam with a built-in microphone.

Scanner

A **scanner** is a device that works a bit like a photocopier. You put the document or picture onto its glass surface and by scanning it, you create a computerized version of the document or picture. This is particularly useful if you have old photographs that you would like to put onto the computer. If you have a digital camera, then you do not necessarily need a scanner. The scanner is just for getting traditional photographs onto your computer. Scanners can also be used to scan any other kind of document as long as it is A4 size or less. If you do get a scanner, make sure it

A flatbed scanner

has at least 1200dpi. This is dots per inch. The higher the number, the clearer the scanned images will be.

Memory stick

These are small **storage devices** that let you store information in a portable way. If you ever need to move information from one computer to another, then you will need a **memory stick**. They are very small and plug into the USB port. You can copy information onto them and then take them with you. For example, if

A memory stick

you go to an evening class and want to take in some work that you did on your home computer, then you can use a memory stick. The amount that a memory stick can store is measured in **megabtyes** (MB) or **gigabytes** (GB). If you think you will be transferring lots of music or video, then you should buy a 1GB or 2GB memory stick. If not, 128MB or above will be adequate.

Speakers

These are just the same as the speakers on your stereo or radio except you plug them into the back of your computer. You will need speakers if you want to play music or videos, or if you want to talk to other people over the Internet, for example, using a web cam. Make sure that you choose speakers that plug into the electricity supply otherwise they will not be loud enough. The amount of volume you can get is measured in watts (W). More watts means more volume.

CD/DVD burner

This allows you to make your own CDs or DVDs. There are many different formats of CD and DVD. A standard CD or DVD will allow you to read information from the disk, but not to put any information back onto it. You might want to be able to create (burn) your own CDs and DVDs. For example, if you take lots of photographs, you could burn them onto a CD to give to family and friends. If you have made a film using a digital camcorder, you might want to burn it onto a DVD. If you think you might want to do this, then you should make sure that you

A CD/DVD tray

get a **CD-R, CD-RW** or **DVD-R** or **DVD-RW**. The R means recordable and the RW means re-writable. You can buy some that plug into a USB port or you can have one put into your base unit/tower.

Summary

In this chapter we have discussed:

- What extra computer equipment (peripherals) you might need
- What 'specification' of peripheral to buy
- Digital cameras, camcorders and web cams
- Scanners
- Memory sticks
- Speakers
- CD and DVD burners

03

programs (software) you might need

In this chapter you will learn:

- what a computer program is
- which computer programs are essential
- what computer programs you might need

Aims of this chapter

Once you have chosen your computer system and any other devices that you might need, you must then select which programs you want on your computer. Programs, or software allow you to use your computer to do all the things you want, such as writing letters, emailing and surfing the Internet. This chapter will explain the most common types of software and look at all the software you might need.

3.1 What software do you need?

Software allows you to do the things you want to do. Without software, you can't do anything with your computer – it is just a pile of useless equipment. There are different types of software, each of which allows you to carry out different jobs on your computer. You may have heard of some already. For example: **word processing** software is needed to type letters and other types of documents; web **browser** software is needed to access the **Internet**; email software is needed to send and receive emails.

So what do you need?

Microsoft®

Microsoft® is the biggest name in standard software. Its owner, Bill Gates, is the richest man in the world. Microsoft® is responsible for Word, Excel®, PowerPoint®, Access, Publisher, Internet Explorer®, Outlook® and Hotmail®, which are some of the most common software used. They also make Windows®. Now you can see why he's the richest man in the world!

Microsoft® Office

This is a collection of different bits of software designed to do different jobs. They come together as a bundle, which makes it cheaper than buying them each individually. Although, you might not want all of the software right now, it is better to buy it as a bundle as it will cost much more to buy it individually later on. It is recommended that you buy the latest version of Microsoft® Office. You will get:

Microsoft® Word

This is word processing software used for typing documents of all types. For example, you can use Word for typing letters, minutes, essays, etc.

Microsoft® Excel®

This is **spreadsheet** software used for handling numbers and calculations. For example, you can use word if you want to keep financial records on your computer.

Microsoft® PowerPoint®

This is used to create **slideshow presentations**. For example, you can use this if you want to make slideshows of your holiday photographs.

Microsoft® Access

This is **database** software used to store records. For example, you could use this to record club members or names and addresses of personal friends.

Microsoft® Publisher

This is desktop publishing software used to create publications of all kinds. For example, you could use this to create posters, flyers or pamphlets.

Microsoft® Outlook®/Outlook Express®

These are both email programs. You can set these up on your computer and send and receive email. However, it is recommended that you use one of the free **web-based** emails referred to later.

Hints and tips
Microsoft® sells different versions of Office. Some of them do not contain all the software listed above. Make sure you get the version you want with the software that you need in it.

Internet Explorer®

This is called a browser and is needed to view all of the information on the Internet. Internet Explorer® (IE) is usually found on any computer that has Windows® on it – so you have probably already got it.

Email

Most email software is web-based. This means that you do not need to buy it as you can use it for free on the Internet. Another advantage of web-based software is that you can use it from anyone's computer – you do not have to use your own. You will get free email from the company that you get your Internet from, known as your Internet Service Provider (ISP).

Internet Service Provider (ISP)

This is a service that gives you access to the Internet. It is basically a telephone service that allows you to get Internet access down your telephone line. This service is provided by a business e.g. BT, NTL, Talk Talk, etc. To get on the Internet, you must have an ISP. There are lots to choose from and they vary in price and the speed at which they work. It is a competitive business so it is worth shopping around and asking family and friends which one they use and whether they are happy with it.

Anti-virus

This software stops your computer getting infected with computer **viruses**. Viruses are small programs written by people with nothing better to do. They attack your computer and can damage it or the information that is on it. Anti-virus software searches your computer for viruses and kills them. If you buy anti-virus software you are entitled to **updates**, which means that you will get new versions of the software that will kill any new viruses.

3.2 Software supplied with devices

Whenever you buy a new device such as a camera or a **scanner**, it will come with a CD or DVD that contains the software for the device. All devices need software to make them work on your computer. The software also includes useful functions. For example, the software that comes with your digital camera will allow you to **browse** and edit your photographs on-screen. The problem with all of this software is that it is different. For example, the software supplied with a Canon camera will be different from that supplied with a Kodak camera.

Having said that, most software conforms to some standard rules, as you will see later. All software should also be supplied with a user manual to help you get started.

3.3 Free software

Generally speaking, you get what you pay for and this is also the case with free software! There is a lot of free software available on the Internet for you to **download**. If you buy a computer magazine, you often get a CD packed with free software. Some of this is genuinely good stuff. For example, software companies often give away older versions of their software to encourage you to buy the latest version. Some free software is free only for 30 days and then you have to buy it – so watch out for this. It will normally run out just after the 30 days without causing any problems. Some free software is free because it's rubbish.

As a rule, it is recommended that you put free software onto your computer only if you think you will be using it. The temptation is to clutter up your computer with all of this stuff because it is free. However, every time you add something to your computer, it does alter the settings, which might cause problems elsewhere. Also, you will end up with a long list of programs making it harder to find the ones you do want to use.

3.4 Licences

Finally, make sure that any free software you use is genuine. It is easy to create copies of software and you may know people who offer you 'free' software. It is illegal to use software that you have not paid for. When you buy legitimate software you get a licence to use it on your computer. In theory, you can be fined heavily for using unlicensed software.

Make sure that you keep the original packaging of all software that you buy, as this is the licence. This also means making sure that you get a copy of Windows® from whomever sold you your computer.

Summary

In this chapter we have discussed:
- The main items of software you will need
  - Microsoft® Office
  - Internet Explorer®
  - Email and anti-virus software
- Software that comes with devices
- Free software

04

getting started – first basics

In this chapter you will learn:

- how to switch your computer on and off
- how to use the mouse and keyboard
- about the Windows® desktop
- how to open and close programs
- how to open and close folders

Aim of this chapter

This chapter takes you from the beginning assuming that you have never switched on a computer before. Even if you have, you might find it useful to work through this chapter on the basics of computer use.

4.1 Switching the computer on and off

To switch your computer on, you need to find the button that has this symbol on it.

This is the on/off button although you should only actually use it to switch the computer on.

Press the on/off button and release – and wait.

The computer will now go through a **start-up routine** that may take a few minutes. If nothing appears on the screen, it may be that the monitor is not switched on. The monitor also has an on/off switch, so make sure that this is on. You can tell that the computer and monitor are on as there is a small (usually green) light that will light up when they are on.

Hints and tips

The start-up routine is carried out by the Windows® operating system that we talked about in Chapter 1. It has to go through this routine every time you switch on. Windows® will also switch the computer off when you tell it to, which is why you never need to use the on/off button to switch your computer off.

When it has finished its routine, you will see the **Windows**®
desktop, which will look something like this:

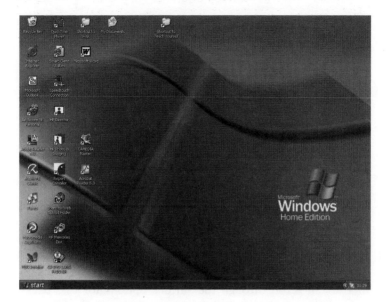

Think of the desktop like a normal desktop – a flat surface with
lots of things on it. You will always start at the desktop and will
use it a lot, so you need to get used to it. The small pictures you
can see are called **icons.** By double clicking on these with the
mouse, you can open up programs and **folders.**

Also, note the 'Start' button in the bottom left-hand corner. This
is often referred to as the Start **menu** and will provide access to
everything on your computer.

The Windows® desktop can be customized. You can move the
icons around and add your own background, called 'wallpaper'.
This means that your desktop might not look exactly the same as
the one shown here. To change your wallpaper:

1 Right click anywhere on the desktop. If you have never used
   a mouse before, please work through sections 4.2 and 4.3.
2 Select 'Properties'.
3 Select 'Desktop'.

The following screen is displayed:

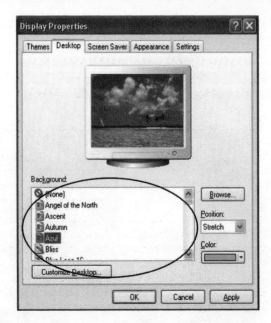

4 You can scroll through the various options for the 'Back-ground' as shown. It will show you a **preview** of what each background will look like.
5 When you have found one you like, click on 'OK'.

4.2 Using the mouse

To make things happen, you can either use the mouse or the keyboard. Your mouse will have at least two buttons called the left and right buttons. It may also have a scroll wheel between the two buttons.

As you move the mouse around on your mouse mat, it will move a small **pointer** on the screen. All programs work with a mouse – you simply point and then click on the icons and menus that you want to use.

Throughout this book, when you need to click on something on the screen, it will be shown in the text in single speech marks. For example, if you need to click on a menu on the screen called Save, the instruction will read: Click 'Save'.

To use the mouse:

1 Hold it lightly using the thumb on one side and your fourth and little fingers on the other. This leaves your second and third fingers free for clicking and using the scroll wheel. You might want to practise moving the mouse around and watching as the pointer moves.

Hints and tips

Some mice are more sensitive than others, which means that the pointer will move by different amounts. If you use more than one computer, it might take a while to get used to a different mouse.

---

2 As well as pushing the mouse around, you will also need to lift it slightly from time to time. The mouse only works if it is flat on your mouse mat, but sometimes you simply run out of mouse mat! When this happens, you need to lift the mouse off the mat and reposition it in the centre of the mouse mat before you start moving it again. This might be a bit tricky when you first start, so have a play until you feel more comfortable with it.

Hints and tips

You can actually move the pointer all the way across the screen without having to move the mouse much at all using the lifting technique described here.

4.3 Clicking on things

There are three types of click:

- A left click (known as a click). This is used mainly when you want to select something from a list or menu.
- A double left click (known as a double click). This is another thing that you might need to practise when you start. A double click is when you click twice on the left button, quite quickly. You use this when you click on icons.
- A right click (known as a right click!). This provides access to hidden menus. Right clicks work only in certain places, as you will start to discover later.

Let's practise the clicks now.

1 First, from the desktop, click (that's a single left click) on 'Start' in the bottom left-hand corner.

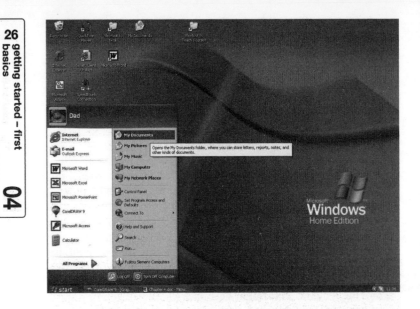

2 Click on 'My Documents'.

This will then show a window that looks a bit like the one below. It is called a window because it opens in a **frame**. Don't worry if yours does not have exactly the same number of little yellow folders in as this, but it should look something like this:

You will notice that there are three small icons in the top right-hand corner of the window. These are displayed in every window in every program that you ever use.

The first one is called **Minimize**. This closes the window but leaves it available so that you can get it back later.

3 Click on the 'Minimize' icon now.

The window closes, but if you look at the bar across the bottom of the screen (called the Windows® taskbar), you will see that it is still available here. This is useful as it means you can have lots of different things open at the same time, and you can use the taskbar to get to them quickly.

4 To re-open the 'My Documents' window, click on it now.

The second icon of the three is called **Restore**. This changes the size of the windows from full screen (where it fills the screen) to a smaller size. The advantage of this is that you can have several smaller windows all open at the same time.

5 Click on the 'Restore' icon now to see what happens.

6 Click on it again to restore it to its original size.

The final icon is the cross. This closes the window. You will use this a lot as this is the main way of closing things down when you have finished with them.

To close this window:

7 Click on the little cross in the very top right-hand corner of the window as shown.

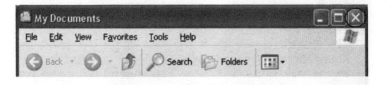

You have now used a double click and a click to open and close a window. You are now back at the desktop.

8 Move the mouse pointer somewhere on the desktop where there are no icons.

9 Right click.

A hidden menu is displayed. This menu will be different depending on where you press the right click.

10 Click somewhere else on the desktop and the hidden menu will disappear again.

Hints and tips

The scroll wheel comes in handy when you are looking at things on the screen that take up more than a screen-full. If this is the case you have to **scroll**, or move up and down. This is where the scroll wheel comes in. We will use this for the first time in Chapter 6.

4.4 Using the keyboard

This is a bit more straightforward as it works in the same way as a typewriter. That is, you press the keys on the keyboard and whatever you type will appear on the screen.

When you are on the desktop you don't really need to type anything, but you will use it a lot in other programs. There are a few keys on the keyboard that carry out specific functions. You will be introduced to these as you need them, but it is worth pointing a few out now.

Throughout this book, when you need to press one of the keys on the keyboard, the name of that key will be shown in capitals. For example, if you need to press the ENTER key, the instructions will read: Press ENTER.

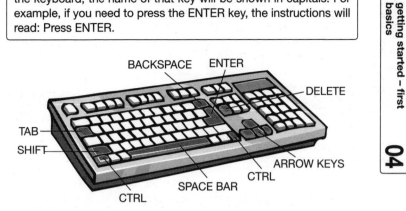

ENTER: You will use this key a lot. It is used to tell the computer you want to do something and is used when typing to start new lines.

SPACE: The space bar is used to add spaces in between words when typing.

TAB: This is really useful when you are filling in forms when you are on the **Internet**. It will move you from one part of the form to the next and saves you having to click.

SHIFT: Allows you to type capitals and gives you access to all of the characters displayed at the top of the keys, for example, above the numbers.

CTRL: Can be used for **shortcuts**. These are ways of doing things quicker. You will be told about these as you work through the book.

BACKSPACE and DELETE: Used a lot when typing. They delete (erase) any characters that you have typed incorrectly.

ARROW KEYS: Can be used like the mouse to move the pointer on the screen around (in some programs).

4.5 Opening and closing programs

Programs are all of those things that you use your computer for, for example, **word processing,** or surfing the Internet. To do these things, you have to open the appropriate program. You open programs from the desktop in one of two ways:

- Double click on the icon that represents the program on the desktop.
- Click on 'Start' and find the program on the list.

Hints and tips

All programs have little pictures associated with them. These are called icons. For example, Microsoft® Word has a blue W and Internet Explorer® has a blue E. There is also a piece of text with the icon that tells you what program it is.

It is easiest to open programs from an icon, but sometimes the icon does not exist, so you have to go through the Start menu. To practise, we are going to open Microsoft® Word. To open from an icon:

1 Double click on the 'Word' icon .
   The Word program will now open and will look like this:

2 To close the program, click on the small cross in the top right-hand corner of the window.

To open from the start menu:

1 Click on 'Start'.

2 Move the mouse pointer to 'All Programs'. A list will now be displayed.
3 Find 'Microsoft Word' in the list and click on it.
   The program will **load**.
4 Click on the cross to close the program.

The process of opening and closing any program is exactly the same. This means there will always be either an icon, or if there is no icon, the name of the program will appear on the list in the Start menu. All programs can be closed by clicking on the cross in the top right-hand corner.

4.6 Opening and closing folders

Folders are where you save your work. When you first start off there is a folder called My Documents which has nothing in it. Think of folders like normal paper folders. They are just somewhere to put your work. All work (whatever it is) is stored in **files**.

Hints and tips
It might help to think of your computer as an electronic filing cabinet. The folders are where you will store all of your work.

Folders have their own icon, which is a little yellow folder! Whenever you see a little yellow folder, it means that there is some work stored in it. Later on, you will make your own folders.

As a practice:

1 From the desktop, double click on the 'My Documents' folder.
2 This will open a new window that will show you all of the work that is stored in this folder. If it's a brand new computer, there will be nothing in it. You will probably see two other folders within this folder, one called My Music and one called My Pictures. This is where you can store music and pictures if you want.
3 Now go to 'Start' in the bottom left-hand corner and open Word again.
   You have now got two things open: My Documents and Word. You are now multi-tasking! This means that you are doing more than one thing at the same time. To switch between the two things that are open, you just click on them in the taskbar as described previously. Try this now.

4 Click on 'My Documents' in the taskbar and then click on the cross in the top right-hand corner of the window to close it.

Word will still be open. Leave it open for now, as we will use it to look at some of the standard features of software.

4.7 Menus and toolbars

This book will introduce you to lots of different **software**. Although each program is used for different things, there are some standard features. This is quite useful because it means once you have learned how to do something in one program, you can transfer that skill to any program. You have already seen one standard feature in that all software opens in a window, and you need to click on the cross to close it.

Two other standard features are that all programs have menus and **toolbars**.

- Menus are lists of options that you can choose from. The options are all of the different things that the software can do.
- Toolbars provide links to all of these same options, but via an icon rather than a menu. In other words, you can click on a little picture of something to make things happen.

As you work through the book, you will be taken through many menu options and be shown many toolbar options. Some of the common ones are listed here. Menus and toolbars are usually shown at the top of the window after you have opened the program. In this example, the menus and toolbar for Word are shown:

- The menus are shown as words e.g. File, Edit, Insert, etc. These menus will vary a bit depending on what program you are using but many of them are the same in all programs.

- The toolbars are all of those small icons (pictures). Each picture represents a different option.

This gives you two ways of doing the same thing. For example, if you wanted to print, you could either click on the 'Print' icon in the toolbar 🖨 or you could click on the 'File' menu and then select 'Print' from the list of options displayed.

The most common icons that you will use are:

☐ Opens a new blank document
📂 Opens an existing document
💾 Saves a document
🖨 Prints a document

4.8 Switching off the computer

You might not want to do this just yet, but it is worth having a practice now. Remember that you don't actually press the on/off button to switch the computer off – that would be far too easy. Instead you do the following:

1 Click on the 'Start' button in the bottom left-hand corner.
2 Select '**Shut Down**'.
3 Select 'Shut Down' again from the options listed.
4 Click 'OK'.

Your computer may take a while to switch itself off, but after a few seconds it will shut itself down.

Hints and tips

It is important that you shut down the computer using this method. It carries out various checks as it shuts down to make sure that it is done properly. Switching off using the on/off key will cause problems when you come to switch on again.

When the computer shuts down it will also turn off the monitor, so you do not need to switch this off separately.

You now need to switch your computer back on again so you can carry on with Chapter 5.

Summary

In this chapter we have discussed:
• How to switch the computer on and shut it down properly
• How to use the mouse
• How to click, double click and right click with the mouse
• How to use the keyboard
• How to open and close programs and folders

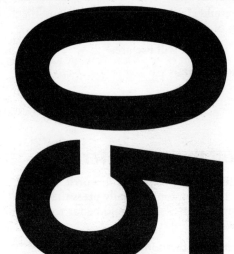

05

getting equipment and programs onto your computer

In this chapter you will learn:

- how to attach equipment to your computer
- how to put new programs onto your computer from CD or DVD
- how to access information stored on a CD or DVD
- about downloading software from the Internet

Aims of this chapter

This chapter will show you how to attach new pieces of equipment such as a printer or scanner to your computer and how to load the programs that are needed to make the equipment work. It will also show you how to install other programs that you might want to add.

Hints and tips

The process of attaching new equipment is often called installing. You can also **install** or **load** new **software**. This is just computer-speak for adding something.

5.1 Installing new equipment

There are many occasions when you need to add a new piece of equipment to your computer. For example, you might want to:

- attach a new printer
- attach a **scanner**
- plug in your digital camera
- add a web cam
- plug in some speakers
- add a new **modem** so you can get onto the **Internet**.

Hints and tips

It is preferable to get your computer set up how you want it when you first buy it. Ask the shop to install the hardware and software for you so that it is ready to use when to get it. Most shops will do this without charging any extra.

The technical term for all of this equipment is **hardware,** and the process of attaching it to your computer and getting your computer to recognize it is pretty much the same regardless of what hardware you are adding.

When you buy new hardware, it will usually come with a set of instructions and a CD or DVD that contains the software or program needed to make it work. The CD or DVD will include an **installation routine.** This is a series of screens that you will be taken through.

The example shown here is for installing a new web cam and although all installation routines will vary slightly depending on what you are installing, you will find that most installation routines are similar to this one.

1 Open the CD/DVD drive on your computer by pressing the button next to it on your computer.
2 Put the CD/DVD that came with your hardware into the drive with the label facing up.
3 Close the CD/DVD drive by pressing the button again.

Hints and tips
The CD/DVD drive will open and close when you press the button once.

---

4 Wait for a few seconds and the CD/DVD will start to play automatically. If it plays automatically, go to step 8; if not, go to step 5.
5 If it does not start playing after a few seconds, click on 'Start' in the bottom left-hand corner, click on 'My Computer', double click the CD/DVD drive as shown:

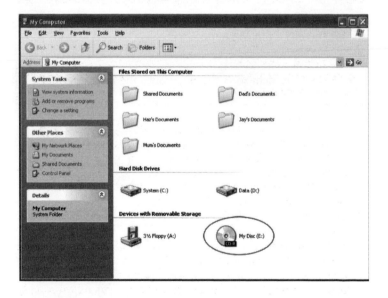

6 The CD/DVD will then open and the contents of the disk will be displayed in a new window.
7 Double click the file named 'Set up'.
8 The installation routine will now open and the first screen will be shown. In this case, it looks like this:

SMART CAM 2.1
For Windows 98, ME, 2000 and XP

Install Camera Driver
Install Smart Cam 2.1
Install Ulead Photo Express
Install Ulead Photo Explorer
Install Ulead Cool 360
Browse CD Contents
EXIT

Hints and tips

Most installation routines have a main **menu** with a number of options on it. Select the one that installs the hardware. This will normally be the first one on the list and will be clearly labelled with the word 'Install' or 'Add'.

The next few screens will vary depending on what you are installing. This process of being led through several screens is called a **wizard**. Wizards often ask you lots of confusing questions, but there is a simple rule: click 'Next'. The wizard will set up the new hardware using standard settings. Clicking the Next button accepts all of these settings.

9 Click on 'Next' until there are no more screens and then click 'Finish'.

Your new hardware is now installed. You may be prompted to switch the computer off and back on again for the new setting to work. You must do this if it tells you to.

10 You can now plug in the new hardware. This will normally be into the **USB port**. Make sure you plug it in with the little USB symbol ⟜ facing up.

After a few seconds, you will see a message on your desktop telling you that new hardware has been found. It is now ready to use.

5.2 Installing new software

There are many occasions when you might need to do this. For example:

- You buy a new piece of hardware that comes with its own program, for example digital cameras are normally supplied with photograph editing software.
- You buy a new program that was not already on your computer.
- You get a free CD from a computer magazine that contains free software.

The process is almost exactly the same as installing new hardware. You will be presented with an installation routine and you will need to follow the wizard to get the new software installed properly.

When you buy software it will be supplied on a CD/DVD. This example shows how to install the software for an **iPod**™, which is called **iTunes**™. Most software uses the same wizard as this.

Hints and tips

An iPod™ is a device that allows you to store thousands of music tracks and listen to them via earphones. They have become popular among all age groups over the last few years. See Chapter 20 for more information.

---

1 Open the CD/DVD drive on your computer.
2 Put the CD/DVD that came with your hardware into the drive with the label facing up.
3 Close the CD/DVD drive.
4 Wait for a few seconds and the CD/DVD will start to play automatically. If it plays automatically, go to step 8; if not, go to step 5.
5 If it does not start playing after a few seconds, click on 'Start' in the bottom left-hand corner, click on 'My Computer', double click the CD/DVD drive as shown on next page.
6 The CD/DVD will then open and the contents of the disk will be displayed in a new window.
7 Double click the file named 'Set up'.

8 The installation routine will now start and a screen will be shown that then disappears.

Hints and tips

When things are installing to your computer you will often be shown a progress bar. This is a visual representation of how long it will take to do its thing. These are quite useful so you know whether to sit and wait, or go for a cup of tea.

The main menu will then be displayed. In this case it looks like this:

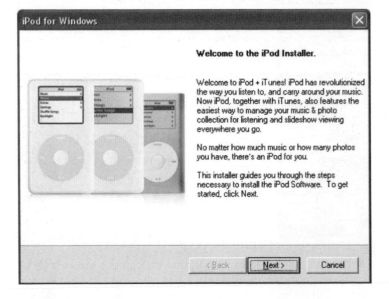

Like all wizards, you are prompted to click the 'Next' button to continue to the next screen. Each screen will present you with a range of options. Although you can change the options, the general rule is to just keep clicking 'Next' until there are no more Nexts left to click, and then you click 'Finish'.

9 Click 'Next' until there are no more, and then click 'Finish'. You will then be shown a screen that tells you that you have successfully installed your new software. It may ask you to switch your computer off and on again. You must do this.

Hints and tips

Switching your computer off and on again is sometimes referred to as a **reboot**. So if you are told to reboot your computer you need to switch it off from the Start menu and then switch it back on again using the on/off button.

---

10 When you have finished installing you can use the software in one of two ways:

- Click on 'Start' in the bottom left-hand corner.
- Click 'All Programs'.
- Click on the new program from the list.

If there are lots of programs installed, it might take you a while to find as illustrated here. It is the iTunes™ software that we have just installed.

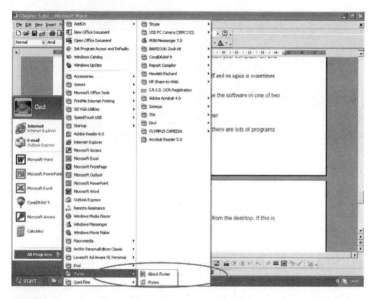

Some installation routines will create a **shortcut** from the desktop. This means that it will put a little **icon** on the **desktop** (see next page) for you so that you can open it from here. If this is the case:

- Go to the desktop.
- Find the icon for the new software.
- Double click on the icon.

This screenshot (overpage) shows the shortcut to the iTunes™ software. It does not matter whether you open the software using the Start menu or the shortcut, they both take you to the same thing.

Hints and tips
Make sure you keep all your CDs and DVDs in a safe place. If your computer ever goes wrong you will need them to install all the hardware and software again. They are also proof that you have bought a legal copy.

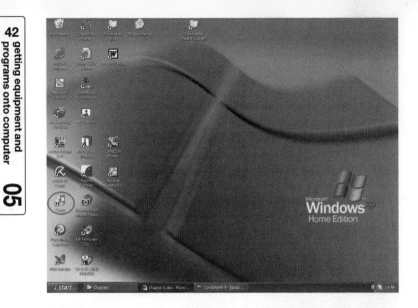

5.3 Accessing information stored on a CD or DVD

So far, you have used a CD or DVD to copy information from the CD or DVD onto your computer. Once you have done this, it means that you do not need to put the CD or DVD in again, as the information that was on the CD/DVD is now on your computer.

There are many occasions where you want to get information from a CD or DVD without actually installing it onto your computer. For example, if you want to watch a movie, or listen to a CD, or access something like an encyclopaedia on CD, you do not have to install as such, you just have to play the CD/DVD.

This process is similar to the one described in section 5.2 in that you insert the CD or DVD into the drive.

1 Insert the CD/DVD that you want to play.
2 The CD/DVD may now **autorun**. This means that it will start to play automatically.

If not:

3 Click on 'Start'.
4 Click on 'My Computer'.
5 Select the CD or DVD drive as shown:

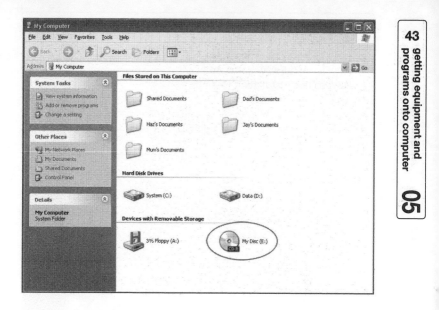

6 On the CD/DVD cover it will tell you what to click on to make the CD/DVD play.

The CD or DVD will now play. If it is something like an **online** encyclopaedia, it will have its own set of menus and you will need to follow the instructions on screen. If it is a music CD or a film DVD, it will start to play automatically using whatever **media player** software you have on your computer.

Hints and tips
There is more information on accessing music and film in Chapter 14.

5.4 Downloading software from the Internet

It is also possible to **download** (copy) software from the Internet. This means that rather than getting the software on CD, it can be transferred from the Internet onto your computer. This is not covered in detail in this chapter, as you need to be familiar with the Internet first. Chapters 10 to 16 cover use of the Internet in much more detail including downloading software.

Summary

In this chapter we have discussed:

- How to install new hardware
- How to install new software
- How to use installation routines
- How to use wizards
- How to load software from the Start menu and from a shortcut
- How to access information on CD or DVD
- Downloading from the Internet

06

writing letters using Microsoft® Word

In this chapter you will learn:

- how to type a letter
- how to save the letter
- how to change the size and style of the font
- how to format the letter
- how to correct mistakes
- how to correct spellings automatically
- how to print

Aims of this chapter

This is the first of the chapters on word processing that will show you how to create and save a letter. It will show you how to change the style of the font (lettering styles) and how to format (layout) the document to make it look like a letter. It also covers other word processing skills such as the use of the automatic spell-checker.

6.1 Getting started in Microsoft® Word

Microsoft® Word is a **word processing** program. This means that it is designed to create all kinds of documents where the main thing that is required is lots of text. This chapter focuses specifically on writing letters and Chapter 7 looks at other types of documents that you might want to create. This is a good place to start as many of the basic computing skills are learned using Word.

Hints and tips

There are other programs that you can use for writing letters but this is the most common. If you want to create specific types of documents such as leaflets or pamphlets then you would be better using Microsoft® Publisher. See Chapters to 21 to 23.

1 First, you need to open Word. To do this you can:

- Find the **shortcut** for it on your **desktop** and double click on it.

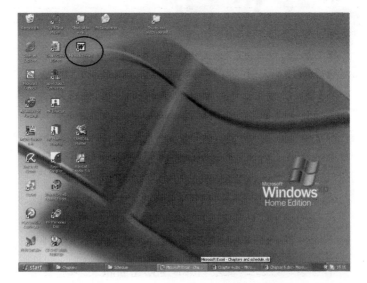

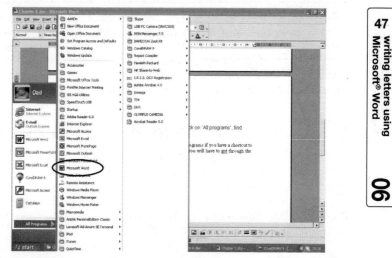

If you do not have a shortcut:

- Click on 'Start' in the bottom left-hand corner, click on 'All Programs', find 'Microsoft Word' and click on it.

Hints and tips

It is much easier to open programs if you have a shortcut to them on your desktop. If you do not have a shortcut, you will have to go through the Start **menu**.

---

2 Word will now open and you will be faced with a screen that looks like this.

The large white space is the page. Think of this as a piece of A4 paper onto which you are going to type your letter.

There are many other things on the screen and it is worth taking some time to understand what they all are.

At the top of the screen:

Title bar	**Menus**	**Toolbars**
Shows the name of the document and the program being used.	Click on these to get access to various options e.g. Print and Save.	These are shortcuts to the menu options. These are quicker to use than the menus.

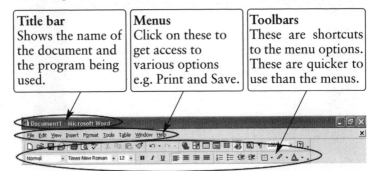

At the bottom of the screen:

Toolbars	**Page information**
There are more toolbars shown down here providing more shortcuts to menu options.	Shows how many pages are in your document and which page you are on.

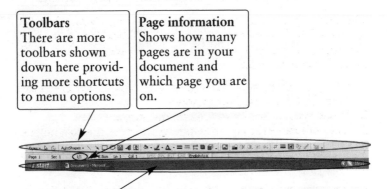

Windows taskbar
This is part of Windows and is always shown, whichever program you are in. It shows all of the programs that are open. At the moment, the only thing open is the Word document. You can access the Start menu at any time to get to other programs. On the right-hand side of the taskbar you can see the time and some small icons. These icons are shortcuts to other programs and we look at this later.

6.2 Scrolling up and down

On the far right-hand side of the screen is the **scroll bar**.

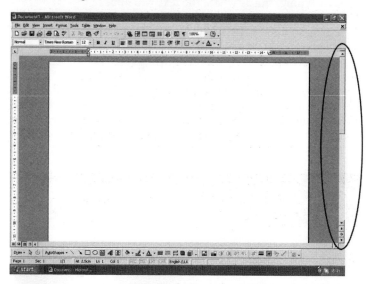

This allows you to move up and down the page, which is called **scrolling**. The darkest grey bar at the top indicates how much of the page you can see on the screen – about half in this case. To move to the bottom half of the screen:

1 Click anywhere in the dark grey section of the scroll bar and hold the left mouse button down.
2 While holding the button, move the mouse down.
3 This will move the page down so you can see the bottom half.

To move the bar back up hold the left mouse button down and move the mouse up.

Hints and tips
You can use the scroll wheel on your mouse here to scroll up and down.

6.3 Typing a letter

To get back to our letter, the first thing that needs typing is the address. You can use your own address here rather than our made-up one!

1 In the top left-hand corner of the white space you will see a small line flashing – this is called the **cursor** I . When you start typing, this is where the text will appear.
2 Type in the first line of the address as shown. For capital letters hold the SHIFT key

as you type the letter. Leave a single space between each line by pressing the SPACE BAR (the wide one at the bottom of the keyboard) once.

3 Press the ENTER key.

This moves the cursor down to the beginning of the next line.
4 Now type the second line of the address and press ENTER.
5 Continue like this until every line of the address has been typed.

At the moment the text is **left-aligned**. This means that it will all line up down an imaginary line on the left-hand side of the page.

Hints and tips

You will notice that there is a white space at the top of the page and down the left-hand side that you cannot type into. These are reserved so that you have a margin when you print out.

When you have finished typing, your document should look like this:

If you have made a mistake, you can correct it at any time. For example, let's pretend that the address was actually 14 Acacia Avenue.

1 Use the mouse to point the cursor just before the 2 (in-between the 1 and 2). If you are not used to using a mouse, this can actually be quite tricky.
2 When you have got the **mouse pointer** between the 1 and the 2, you need to click once. This puts the cursor between the 1 and the 2.

> Mr John Smith
> 1|2 Acacia Avenue
> Monkton
> Steffleshire
> SE 1 1AA

3 Press the DELETE key once. This will delete the letter or number that is to the right of the cursor – the 2 in this case.

4   Now type in a 4 so that the new address reads 14 Acacia Avenue.

You might want to experiment with moving the cursor and deleting and adding text. You can also use the BACKSPACE key to delete text. This deletes letters to the left of the cursor.

We now have the address, but it is on the wrong side of the page. It needs to be **right-aligned**, which means that it will line up to an imaginary line on the right-hand side of the page. This involves **highlighting** (or selecting) all of the text – this involves a new skill with the mouse.

1   Point the mouse so that the cursor is just to the bottom-right of the address.
2   Now click and hold down the left button.
3   Still holding on to the left button, move the mouse up to the top left-hand side of the address.

    You will notice that the text becomes highlighted as shown in the diagram. This is sometimes called **dragging**.

> **Hints and tips**
> Highlighting text like this is really useful because it means that you
> can work with whole blocks of text rather than just a letter or a
> number at a time. However, it is also a tricky manoeuvre with the
> mouse and might take a bit of practice.

4 Once you have highlighted the text, you can let go of the left
  mouse button.
5 To move the highlighted text to the right, click on the 'right-
  align' button on the **toolbar**:

The block of text will now move to the right. The rest of the
letter needs to be left-aligned so:
6 Click to the right-hand side of the last line of the address
  (after the postcode).
7 Press the ENTER key once.
8 Click the 'left-align' button on the toolbar.

The cursor moves back to the left and you can continue to
type your letter. This means typing in the address of the
person you are sending the letter to, the date, the salutation,
the main body of the letter and the sign-off. The image on
next page shows a standard letter. Notice how a line has been
left between different parts of the letter. You can do this by
pressing ENTER twice at the end of the line.

> **Hints and tips**
> When you get to the end of the line, you do not need to press
> ENTER to start a new line. Word will **wrap** the text for you. This
> means that when it runs out of space on the line, it will automat-
> ically start typing on the line below. The only time you need to press
> ENTER is when you want to start a new paragraph or leave a line.

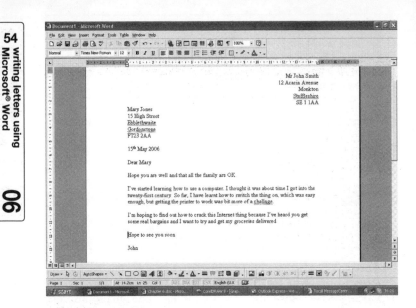

6.4 Saving the letter

When you are working on your computer you need to save your work on a regular basis. This is very important. If you do not save your work regularly you could lose everything you have done, which is frustrating. This applies to everything that you do, not just Word.

There is a **folder** already set up on your computer called My Documents. For now, you should save everything you do into this folder.

Hints and tips

It is possible to lose your work accidentally perhaps by closing a program, or by deleting the wrong thing. You should save your work every 10 minutes to be on the safe side.

To do this:

1 Click on the 'Save' **icon** in the toolbar

2 The following screen will be displayed:

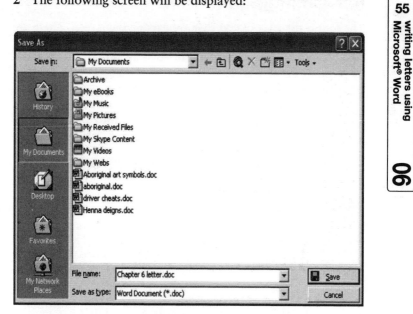

3 Everything that is saved goes into what is called a **file**. You must give every file a name so that you know what is in it. In the box where it says 'File Name' you can now give a name to the document. Type in 'Chapter 6 letter' and press ENTER.

Hints and tips

Try to give all of your files sensible names. You might want to come back to this letter in a few weeks time, so you will need a name that explains what is in it. If you call your file Document1 then you will not remember what is in it.

The document is now saved permanently. You will be able to come back to this document at any time, as it will just stay in this folder forever (or until you choose to delete it).

Next time you save the file, you will not be asked for the name again, it will just save the changes you have made using the same name. Every time you click on 'Save' therefore, it saves the latest version of the file.

6.5 Changing the font

The **font** is the style of text that appears on the screen. There are hundreds of different styles and sizes to choose from, and you can add other features to the font such as underline, **bold** and italic.

For example:

This font is called Times New Roman and it is in 'point size' 12.

This is what it looks like in **bold**, underlined and *italic*.

This one is called Arial, also in size 12, and this is size 14 and this is 18.

Most of the time you need only one or two fonts and if you are typing letters, **point size** 12 is usually fine. The standard setting is Times New Roman size 12 and that is what your letter is.

To change the font:

1 Highlight the whole letter using the method that you used to highlight the address earlier.

Hints and tips

If you hold down the CTRL key and press the letter A at the same time, this will highlight all the text automatically without having to use the mouse. This is an example of a **hot key**. This means you can press strange combinations of keys to get things to happen. There will be more of these as we go through.

---

2 Click on the little arrow to the right of where it currently says Times New Roman.

3 Select 'Arial' from the list that is displayed. All of the text will now change to the Arial font.

6.6 Checking the spelling

You may notice as you type that some of the words have red squiggly lines underneath them and some might have green squiggly lines under them. These are where you have used words that the computer's dictionary does not recognize:

- The red lines indicate spellings that it does not recognize.
- The green lines indicate mistakes that it thinks you have made with your grammar (cheeky thing).

Red lines do not mean that you have necessarily spelled the word wrong. It just means that the computer does not recognize it. This might be because the word is a name, or an English spelling of a word that it wants to spell in American! You can just ignore the red lines – they will not print. However, if the word is spelled wrong you can either:

1 Move the cursor to the word, click, press the DELETE key to delete wrong letters or the whole word, and retype.

OR

2 Right click on the word and you will be given suggested spellings as shown in the diagram.

Hope you are well and that all the family are OK.

I've started learning how to use a computer. I thought it was about time I got into the twenty-first century. So far, I have learnt how to switch the thing on, which was easy enough, but getting the printer to work was bit more of a cha|lnge.

I'm hoping to find out how to crack this Internet thing because I'v
some real bargains and I want to try and get my groceries delivere

challenge
challenger
challenged
challenges

Ignore All
Add

AutoCorrect ▶
Language ▶
Spelling...

Hope to see you soon

John

3 If the correct spelling is on the list you can click on it and the incorrect word will be replaced with the one you have chosen.
4 If the correct spelling is not shown, you will need to click back in the letter and retype the word as described in step 1.

> **Hints and tips**
> You can add words to the computer's dictionary by clicking on 'Add' in the list. If you do this, the next time you use the word, it will be recognized.

6.7 Printing the document

You can print out any document that you create. A printout is a paper copy of what you see on the screen. When you are typing in Word, the white space on the screen represents a piece of A4 paper. Therefore, what you see on the screen is what you will get when you print out. However, the dimensions of the screen are not big enough to view the whole page so you need to use **Print Preview** to be able to see the whole document.

1 Click on the 'Print Preview' icon:

This will then display a screen that shows how the printout will look.

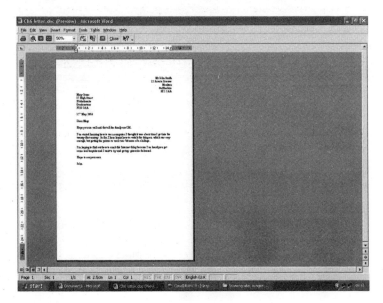

In this case, you can see that all of the text fits easily onto the A4 page.

2   Click on the 'Close' button on the menu at the top.

Village Hall Meeting Minutes.doc (Preview) - Microsoft Word

File   Edit   View   Insert   Format   Tools   Table   Window   Help

51%   Close

3   Now click on the 'Print' icon.

Document1 - Microsoft Word

File   Edit   View   Insert   Format   Tools   Table   Window   Help

Normal   Times New Roman   12   B   I   U   100%

4   After a few seconds your document will start to print.

6.8 Closing the document

When you have finished with a document you need to close it.

1   Make sure that you have saved the **file** as described earlier.
2   Click on the small cross in the top right-hand corner of the screen.

This will close down the document and the Word program and take you back to the desktop.

Summary

In this chapter we have discussed:

- Using Word to type a letter
- Using the cursor
- Highlighting blocks of text
- The Word toolbars and menus
- The Windows® taskbar
- Right and left alignment
- Changing font style and sizes
- Underline, bold and italics
- Checking spellings
- Printing the document
- Closing the program

07

writing minutes and other types of documents

In this chapter you will learn:

- how to create a heading for a document
- how to use bullet points and numbered points
- how to cut and paste text
- how to copy and paste text
- how to delete blocks of text
- how to undo and redo
- how to add an image to a document
- more about printing

Aims of this chapter

This is the second chapter on word processing that will develop and extend the skills you learned in the previous chapter. It will show you how to change the layout for different types of documents, in this case minutes from a meeting. It introduces the idea of cutting, copying and pasting text so you can move text around without having to retype it. You will also be shown how to add images to your documents and how to have more control over what is printed out.

7.1 Adding a heading to a document

Most documents that you type need to have a heading to tell the reader what the document is. Microsoft® Word can be used for typing any kind of document.

For example:

- Minutes from a meeting (the example used in this chapter).
- Your great unfinished novel.
- An essay for a course you are taking.
- Lists of instructions or things to do.

All of these will need headings and even subheadings. These need to stand out from the rest of the text and the way to do this is by changing the **font** (style of typing) and the alignment (where the text is positioned).

In this example, we will put the heading in **bold** and will centre it in the middle of the page.

1 Open Word.
2 Type the following text 'Village Hall Meeting Minutes June 2006'.
3 Now **highlight** the text. There are two ways of doing this here.
   - You could hold the left mouse key and **drag** the **mouse pointer** across the text as described in the previous chapter.

   OR

   - You can move the mouse to the left-hand side at the beginning of the line as shown in the diagram. Notice how the mouse pointer has changed to an arrow.

Village Hall Meeting Minutes

- Click once and the whole line will be highlighted.
4 Now make the heading bold by clicking on the 'Bold' **icon B** and increase the size of the font to 14 by clicking on the little arrow to the right of the 12, and then selecting 14 from the list:

5 Now centre the title by clicking on the 'centre align' icon:

6 Now press ENTER twice. This will move the **cursor** down two lines.
7 Click on the 'left-align' icon to move the cursor back to the left-hand side.

7.2 Using bullet points and numbered points

We can now continue with the rest of the document. Let's say there were five items on the agenda for the meeting:

1   Type in the following five items, pressing ENTER after each one:

Apologies
Village Hall bookings for July
Fundraising events
Progress of the roof repairs
Any other business

2   As this is a list, we can use either bullet points or numbered points to show this.

•   This is a **bullet point**
1   This is a **numbered point**

3   Highlight the list of five items by holding the left mouse button and dragging the mouse pointer over the text.
4   If you want bullet points, click the 'bullet point' icon. For a numbered list click the 'numbered points' icon.

Your list will be changed so that it has either bullets or numbers on it.

5   Save your work at this point. Name the **file**: Village Hall Meeting Minutes.
6   Click underneath the list so that you can continue typing the minutes. We have made up some text as shown in the image on next page.
7   Highlight the subheadings and make them bold.

Hints and tips
You can see that the use of bold is quite effective in making things stand out. You can also use *italics* and underline. However, you only really need to use *one* of these three methods to make things stand out.

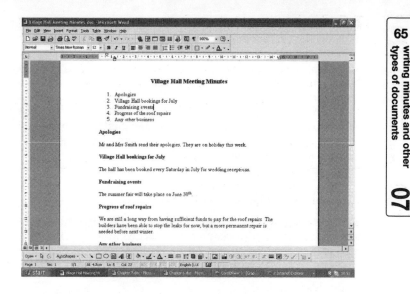

7.3 Cutting and pasting text

One big advantage of computers is that anything you do can be edited. This means that things can be changed without having to start all over again. For example, if you wanted to move some text from one part of the document to another, you can do this without having to retype the text. This is called **cut and paste**. You cut the text from one place and paste it to another.

In this example, we will move the second sentence of the paragraph titled 'Progress of roof repairs' so that it is before the first sentence.

1 Highlight the text that you want to move. In this case, it is the whole of the second sentence.

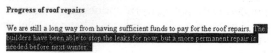

2 Now right click and then click on 'Cut' from the **menu** that is displayed.
3 Move the mouse and click so that the cursor is just to the left of the first sentence as shown:

> **Progress of roof repairs**
>
> |We are still a long way from having suffici
> builders have been able to stop the leaks fo
> needed before next winter.

4 Now right click and then click on 'Paste' from the menu that is displayed. The highlighted text will now move before the first sentence.

Hints and tips

You can use cut and paste to move any amount of text from one place to another. A variation is to **copy and paste**. To do this you choose 'Copy' instead of 'Cut'. This duplicates the highlighted text (makes a copy of it), rather than moving it.

7.4 Deleting blocks of text

A similar technique can be used to delete (get rid of) whole blocks of text. In the previous chapter you learned how to delete single letters at a time using the DELETE and BACKSPACE keys. However, you may wish to delete larger blocks of text.

To do this:

1 Highlight the block of text that you want to delete. Use the same method as described previously.
2 Press the DELETE key. The text will now disappear.

7.5 Undo and redo

It is quite common to make mistakes when using a computer. Sometimes you add something you didn't mean to and sometimes you delete something you didn't mean to (which is much worse).

There is a 'get out of jail card' and it's called **Undo**. This does exactly what it says – if you click on it, it undoes the last thing you did. If you click on it again, it undoes the thing before that – and so on. It is particularly useful if you have just deleted something by mistake.

To undo the deleting that we have just done:

Click on the 'Undo' button:

This will undo the delete.

> **Hints and tips**
> You can use undo in all programs, not just Word. You can also use **Redo**, which is the button to the right of Undo. This re-does whatever you did last.

7.6 Adding images to your document

There are different methods for adding in images to your documents. This chapter focuses on the use of **ClipArt**. There is more about working with images in Chapters 21 to 23 and 27.

ClipArt is available in all Microsoft® **software** and is a library of images. Most of these are cartoon-style images, but some photographs are available too.

To insert an image from ClipArt:

1 Click in your document, where you want your picture to be displayed.
2 Click 'Insert' from the menus across the top.
3 Select 'Picture' and then select 'ClipArt'.
4 The ClipArt library will now open:

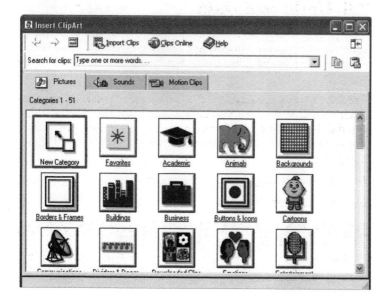

5   You can now **browse** through the categories by **scrolling** through and clicking on the ones you are interested in. You will be shown images that are available.

OR

6   You can use the 'Search for clips' box at the top to type in what you are looking for. For example, type 'roof' into the **search** box and press ENTER.

There is also an option called 'Clips Online' just above the 'Search for clips' option. Clicking on this will link you to a **website** where many more ClipArt images are available.

A list of images related to roofs is now shown. The images will vary from computer to computer depending on what version of ClipArt is installed.

7   When you have found the image you want, click on it and then a small menu will be displayed.

8   Click on the top icon as shown and the image will be added to your document.

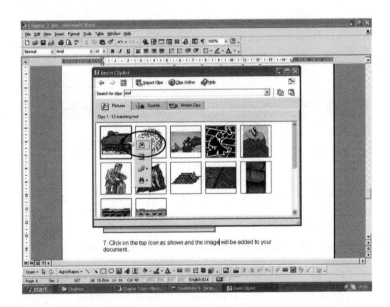

7. Click on the top icon as shown and the image will be added to your document.

7.7 Printing your document

In the previous chapter, you learned how to click on and use **Print Preview** and how to click on the 'Print' icon to get a document to print. There are quite a few other printing options available. Two of the most useful are telling the printer to print in either colour or black and white, and printing several copies of the same document.

To access these options:

1 Click on 'File' and select 'Print' from the menus at the top.
2 This screen will now be displayed:

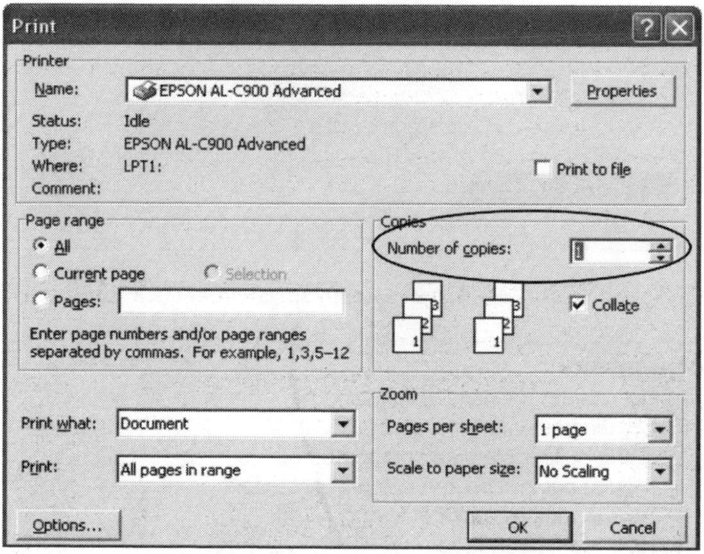

3 To print several copies of the same document, type the number that you want in the box labelled 'Number of copies'.
4 Then click 'OK'.

To select whether you want to print in colour or black and white:

1 Click on 'Properties'. The screenshot shown overleaf is then displayed. Your screen may look slightly different from this but will have the same options.

2   Select 'Color' or 'Black' as appropriate and click 'OK'.

Summary

In this chapter we have discussed:

- Creating a heading for a document
- Using bullet points and numbered points
- How to cut and paste/copy and paste text
- How to delete blocks of text
- How to undo and redo
- How to add an image to a document
- More about printing

08

keeping in touch using email

In this chapter you will learn:

- what email is
- how to set up and use web-based email software
- how to read and reply to emails
- how to send emails
- how to add people to your email address book

Aims of this chapter

This chapter introduces email and covers the basics of sending and receiving emails and how to reply to emails that have been sent to you. It shows you how to make and use an address book of contacts.

8.1 Email software

There are two main types of email **software**. The first is software such as Microsoft Outlook® or Outlook Express®, which come as part of the Microsoft® Office package. These are already installed on your computer and you run them from your **desktop** in the same way as other programs.

The second type is what is called **web-based** email. With these, you do not need to have email software on your computer, as you can get access to it using the **Internet**. Web-based email is generally free. For example, Microsoft Hotmail® is a free-to-use web-based email. You may also be given free email addresses from your Internet Service Provider (the company you get your Internet connection from). For example, BT, AOL and Tiscali all provide free web-based email.

It does not really matter which one you choose. You might find it easier to use one of the web-based ones first as you will not need to set up any software to get it to work.

This chapter will use Hotmail® as an example and will show you how to set up and use an **email account**. All email software works slightly differently although they all have the same basic functions. Therefore, even if you do not use Hotmail®, the basic principles described here will apply. If you already have an email address, then you can skip the section on setting up an email account.

8.2 Email basics

Email stands for electronic mail and the easiest way to think of it is as an electronic letter. You do not have to print it out and send it – instead, it is sent electronically over the Internet. Therefore, you *must* have Internet access in order to use email.

Like normal mail, emails are sent and received using addresses. All email addresses follow the same format. For example:

glynishubblethwaite@hotmail.co.uk

The bit before the @ sign is usually used to identify the individual, and the bit after is the name of the **email provider**.

> **Hints and tips**
> Email has been around for many years now and has millions of users. Therefore you might not get the email address you would like as there is probably already someone out there with the same name as you who has already bagsied the address.

8.3 Setting up an email address in Hotmail®

> **Hints and tips**
> Skip this section if you already have an email address.

First you will need to log on (get on) to the Internet.

1 Click on 'Start'.
2 Click on 'Internet Explorer'.

> **Hints and tips**
> When you **load** Internet Explorer®, it will load your **home page**. The home page can be set to any page you like and to start with, will be set to whatever the shop set it to when you bought it. It might also be set to the home page of your Internet Service Provider (e.g. AOL, BT, Tiscali, etc.).

3 In the **address bar** near the top of the screen (shown below), type 'www.hotmail.com' and press ENTER.

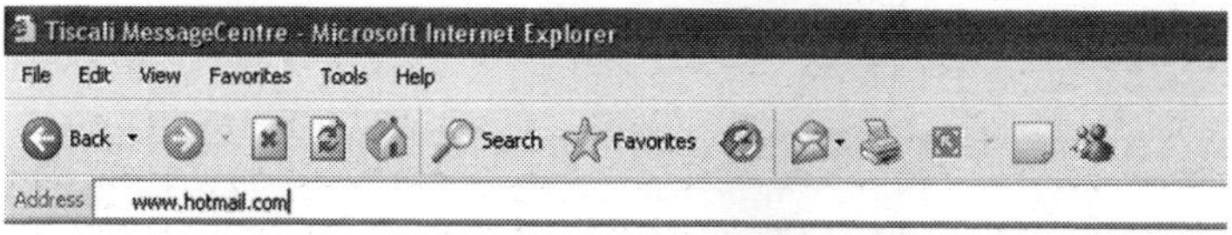

After a few moments the Hotmail® home page will be displayed. This is their main page. There are hundreds of other pages that lead off from this one.

4   Click on the **link** to 'Sign Up' as shown below.

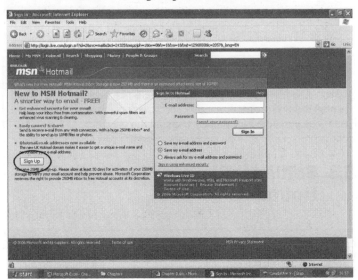

Hints and tips

Web pages like this one contain lots of links to other pages, also
known as **hyperlinks**. This means that you click on the link and it
will take you to another web page.

---

5   On the next screen make sure that you click on the free email
    option. Hotmail® does offer extra services, but these cost
    money.

Hints and tips

Web pages are constantly changing so the pictures of screens that
you seen here might be different by now. If this is the case, the
same or similar options will still be available to you. They might just
be in a different place on the screen.

---

6   You are now asked to complete a form on the screen. This
    may take quite a while, especially if you have never filled in
    an **online** form before. You will find that as you use the
    Internet more, you will be asked to fill in lots of forms. This
    is because the websites want you to register your details with
    them before you can use their free services.

There is guidance available at each stage. You will be asked what email address you would like. This can be anything you like but you might find someone already has the name you want. You need to type this in lower case letters with no spaces in between words e.g. snugglekiss@hotmail.com rather than Snuggle Kiss@hotmail.com

---

Hints and tips
Bear in mind that you will be giving your address out so that people can email you. Therefore, snugglekisses@hotmail.com might seem like a good idea now, but might be a bit embarrassing when you send an email to the vicar!

---

7 You will also be asked for a **password**. Choose something that is easy to remember.
8 Complete the rest of the form and follow the instructions on the screen. If you go wrong or miss anything out, you will be asked to do those bits again.
9 When you have filled in the form, you need to click on the 'I accept' button at the bottom to accept the Hotmail® terms and conditions. You might need to **scroll down** to get to the bottom of the page.
A screen will then be displayed informing you that your email address is ready to use.

Hints and tips
The first time you use Hotmail® it tries to subscribe you to lots of email services. You can have a read through to see if you want any of them, but you don't have to subscribe to any. To move on without subscribing, scroll all the way to the bottom and click 'Continue'.

8.4 Reading an email

To read an email:

1 Open your email software. In this case we are using Hotmail® so:

- Click on 'Start'.
- Click on 'Internet Explorer' and wait a few seconds for the Internet to load.

- Type 'www.hotmail.com' into the address bar as shown.

The Hotmail® home page will then load and will look like this:

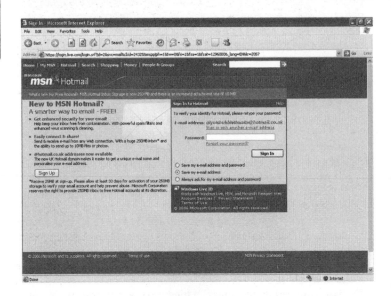

2   Your email address should already be shown. If not, type it in the box next to 'E-mail address' and type in your password and click 'Sign In'.

Hints and tips

The process of opening your email software might be slightly different if you are not using Hotmail®.

---

3   Click on 'My Messages'. In your email software, this might be called the 'Inbox'.
Your **Inbox** is where any email that has been sent to you will be kept. It will show you how many messages you have got,

who they are from, how many of them you have already read and how many are new.

The image below shows the Inbox of a Hotmail® account. Yours may look slightly different but will have all of the same features. This shows one unread message(s).

4   To read a message, double click on it and the whole message will be displayed.
5   When you have read the message you can go back to the Inbox by clicking on the link to it as shown. You can then read your other messages. The Inbox is usually on the left-hand side of the screen.

8.5 Replying to an email

If you want to reply to an email:

1   Open your email software and open the message as described above.
2   After you have read the message, click on 'Reply'.
3   This will automatically set your screen up to send an email back to this person. You do not have to type in their email address as this has been done for you.
    The Hotmail® screen looks like the one overpage and yours will look similar. You can see there is a box with the address

of the person to whom you are replying. The original message is still shown in the main box and you can type your message in above it.

Hints and tips

You may receive a lot of junk email. This is called **spam** and is usually from companies trying to sell you things. The best bet is to simply ignore this and delete it using the 'Delete' option. There is more information on Internet security in Chapter 16.

---

4 Type in your reply. The box that you are typing into works just like Microsoft® Word. You type in, pressing ENTER to leave lines for new paragraphs.
5 When you have finished, click on 'Send'.
   Your email is then sent to the other person's Inbox and they will receive it next time they check their emails.

8.6 Sending an email

To send an email, you need to know the address of the person you are sending it to. Apart from that, it is similar to replying to an email as described in the previous section.

1   Open your email software as described earlier.
2   Click on 'New'. In your email software this might be called 'New Message', 'Create Mail' or 'Compose'.
    When you click on this you will be presented with a screen that allows you to address, type and send the email. In Hotmail® it looks like this:

3   In the 'To:' box, type the email address of the person you want to send the email to.

Hints and tips
Make sure you type the email address accurately or your email will not get through. To get the @ sign you will need to press the SHIFT key with the single comma (').

---

4   The 'Cc:' box allows you to type in another address. If you want to send the same message to two people at the same time, you can put a second address in here. This can be left blank.
5   The 'Bcc:' box allows you to send a blind copy to a third person. This means that they will get a copy of the message, but the person to whom you cc'd it will not know that they got a copy. This can be left blank.

6 The 'Subject:' box is so that the person receiving the message knows what it is about. They will see this before they read the full message so it worth putting something in here.

7 The main box is for the body of the message. You can type as much as you like in here. It works just like Microsoft® Word really – you just keep typing, pressing ENTER when you want to leave a line for a new paragraph.

If you are typing a long email, you might want to use the 'Save Draft' option. This saves what you have typed so far so that you can get it back if something goes wrong before you get the chance to send it. There is a 'Draft' **folder** underneath your Inbox where the drafts will be saved to.

8 When you have finished your message, click on 'Send'.

8.7 Using the address book

You can put any addresses that you want to use into an **address book**. This is just like a normal address book. The advantage of using this is that you don't need to remember all those funny email addresses with the @ sign in them.

In Hotmail® and some other email software, the address book is called 'Contacts'.

1 In your email software, click on 'Contacts'. It may be called 'Address Book' or 'Addresses'.

2 Click 'New'. It might be called 'New Contact'.

3 You can now type in the email address and other details of your contacts. Type email addresses carefully.

4 Now when you want to send an email to anyone in your address book, rather than typing their name into the 'To' box, you just click on the word 'To' itself and your address book will be displayed. You can then select the name from the list.

Summary

In this chapter we have discussed:

• What email is
• How to set up and use web-based email software
• How to read and reply to emails
• How to send emails
• How to add people to your email address book

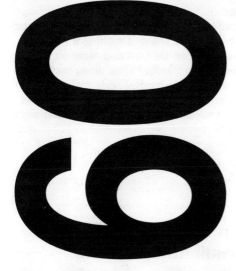

09

sending and receiving pictures and other attachments using email

In this chapter you will learn:

- how to open an email attachment
- how to save an email attachment on your computer
- how to send an email attachment

Aims of this chapter

This chapter is all about email attachments. Anything that can be stored on a computer, be it a document, a picture, a movie or music is stored in a file. Files can be sent and received using email. This is done by attaching the file to the email message, hence the term 'attachments'. This chapter uses pictures, and more specifically photographs, as an example of how to send and receive attachments using email, although you can attach any type of file.

This chapter covers sending and receiving attachments. It assumes that you already have some photographs on your computer that you want to send. If not, you should refer to Chapters 17 to 19 first.

9.1 Opening email attachments

When you receive an email message, if there is anything attached to it, you will see the following symbol *✦* .

Hints and tips

There are lots of different types of email, but they all use this symbol to show that there are **attachments**.

1 Open your email software in the normal way.
Like the previous chapter, we are using Hotmail®, so your email software might look a bit different from this. However, all of the options will be virtually the same, but they might look different on the screen.

2 Look for the paper clip symbol. If there is one, it means that the email has an attachment. In the example on next page top, Albert has received an email with an attachment from his friend Glynis Hubblethwaite.

3 Open the email by clicking on it. The full message is then displayed and the attachments are listed as shown on next page bottom.
In this example there are two **files** attached. One is called Holiday villa 1.jpg and the other is called Holiday villa 2.jpg. The **jpg** part tells you what kind of file it is. A jpg file is a photograph. You will start to recognize these three-letter codes as you use your computer more and more.

Hints and tips

Notice how the two files in this example have slightly different names. Your computer will not let you give two files exactly the same name.

Some email **software** will show you the attachments underneath the text of the email. If this is the case, you can **scroll down** to view the attachments. If not:

4 To open the attachment, click on it.

Depending on your software, different things might happen now. In Hotmail®, and some other email, the software will scan the file to check for **viruses**. Viruses are programs created by people with nothing better to do. They attach themselves to emails and if they infect your computer they can cause it a lot of damage.

If your software does not have a **virus checker**, the attachment will open. In this case, it will display the photograph of a holiday villa.

Hints and tips

Make sure that you have anti-virus software on your computer. See Chapter 16 for more advice on this.

---

5 In Hotmail®, you have to click on 'Download' before the picture is displayed.

6 Once you have viewed the picture, click on the cross in the top right-hand corner of the window that is displaying it.

7 Now click on 'Back' at the top of the screen to get back to the email message.

You can now view the other attachment in the same way.

Hints and tips

There may be many files attached to an email and you will need to go through each of them one by one to view them.

9.2 Saving email attachments

The email attachments are currently attached to the email that they were sent with. If you delete the email, you will also delete the attachments. In this case, it would mean that we would no longer have these photographs.

If you want to keep a copy of the attachments, you need to save them onto your computer. You already have a **folder** called My Pictures and this is as good a place as any to put them.

Hints and tips
You can make your own folders to save files into if you want to. This is explained in Chapter 19.

To save an attachment:

1 When the picture is displayed, click on 'File' in the top left-hand corner of the window that is displaying the picture.
2 Click on 'Save As'.
3 Click on the small arrow to the right of where it reads 'Look in' as shown in the diagram. The following window will then be displayed.

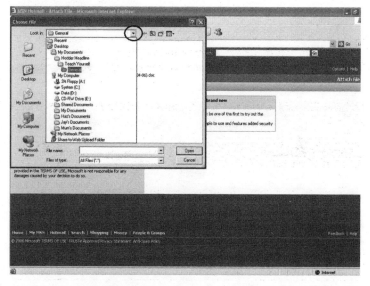

This list is all of the places on your computer where you can save files. The 'Look in' box shows you where it will save this file. If it is already set to My Pictures, you can go on to step 6. If not,
4 Find 'My Documents' and click on it.

5   Find 'My Pictures' and click on it.
6   Click on 'Save'.

The picture is now saved into your My Pictures folder.

Repeat the same process for each attachment.

9.3 Sending an attachment

If you want to send an attachment, you first need to know the name of the file that you want to attach, and the name of the folder that it is in. In this example, we will show the process that Glynis went through when she attached the two pictures of the villa and sent them to Albert. The two files that she sent were called Holiday villa 1.jpg and Holiday villa 2. jpg and were in her My Pictures folder.

1   Open up your email software.
2   Type in the address, subject and message in the usual way.
    You are now ready to add your attachment:
3   Click on 'Attach'. It might have a slightly different name in other email software. It might be called 'Insert' or 'Insert Attachments' or 'File Attachments' or just 'Attachments'.

4   Select 'Pictures'.

You can now see **thumbnail** views of the photographs in the My Pictures folder.

5 Click in the small box in the top left-hand corner of each thumbnail to attach them to your email.

6 Then click on 'Attach Files'.

These files are now attached to the email.

7 Click 'Send' in the usual way.

Your email and the attachments will now be sent to the email address that you typed in.

Hints and tips

Different files are different sizes. Size refers to how much space they take up inside the computer. Photographs can get quite big. This means that they might take a while to attach themselves.

9.4 Attaching different types of file

We have attached photographs in this case, but you can attach any type of file in exactly the same way described above. We were using pictures so the files were saved into the My Pictures folder that is already set up on your computer.

To send other file types you just need to know what they are called (the file name) and where they are (the folder name).

For example, you might want to send a copy of the Village Hall meeting minutes to someone. This is a Word file and is stored in the My Documents folder.

1 Follow exactly the same process as before, but rather than looking in 'My Pictures' when you see this screen, look in 'My Documents'.

2 Find the file called 'Village Hall Meeting Minutes' and double click on it. This file is now attached to the email.

Summary

In this chapter we have discussed:

• How to send email attachments
• How to open email attachments
• How to save email attachments
• How to attach different types of file

10 finding what you need on the Internet

In this chapter you will learn:

- what the Internet is
- how to type in a web address
- what a hyperlink is and how to follow one
- how to move forward and back through web pages
- how to use a search engine
- how to assess whether a website is reliable
- what to do when websites don't work
- adding websites to your 'favourites' list

Aims of this chapter

The main aim of this chapter is to help you to search the Internet to find what you want. It will also give advice on how to work out whether the information you find is reliable and trustworthy. This is the first of seven chapters covering various aspects of the Internet. It is recommend that you should work through this one before attempting the others.

10.1 What is the Internet?

The **Internet** is a worldwide connection of computers. It is also referred to as the **World Wide Web** and is made up of millions and millions of pages of information. These pages are called **web pages**. A collection of web pages is called a **website**. All sorts of organizations and individuals might create a website. In many cases these are businesses trying to sell things, but also includes government organizations, charities, clubs and private individuals.

This presents a couple of problems. The first is that there is so much information available that it can be difficult to find what you need. The second is that there is an awful lot of rubbish in among the good stuff.

Hints and tips

The Internet or net refers to the global connection of computers. The World Wide Web or web refers to all of the information that is available on the Internet. The two terms basically mean the same thing.

10.2 Finding information you need when you know the web address

The easiest way to find a website is if you know the **address**. Website addresses are unique, so no two websites can have exactly the same name. Most organizations advertise their web addresses and include them in their advertising. For example: www.oxfam.org.uk

Hints and tips

Internet Explorer ® is what is known as a web **browser** that allows you to look at websites. Internet Explorer® is the most common but there are other web browsers available such as Mozilla Firefox®, Opera and Netscape®. These work in exactly the same way, but look slightly different.

To go to a website if you know the address:

1 Double click on the 'Internet Explorer' **icon** from your **desktop**.

If you have not got one, click on 'Start' and select it from there. Internet Explorer® will now **load** and a web page will be displayed. This is known as your **home page** and is always the first page to be shown. In this case, the home page is MSN®, which is the Microsoft® home page. Yours might be something completely different.

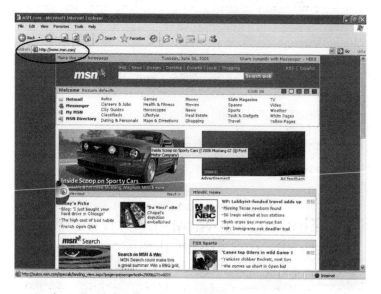

At the top of the page you can see the **address bar** labelled 'Address'.

2 Type in the address. In this case www.oxfam.org.uk
It is important that you type the address exactly as shown with the correct slashes and full stops where relevant.

3 Press ENTER. After a few seconds, you will be taken to the page with the address that you have just typed in.

When you get to the page, it is probably the home page of the website. A home page is the main page of a website. This should contain general information that welcomes you to the site and tells you about the organization or person who is responsible for the site.

Once you are in the website, you may need to move to other parts of the website to find what you want. Nearly all web pages include **links** to other pages. These links are called **hyperlinks**. They might take you to another page on the same website, or to a page on another website.

Hyperlinks can be attached to anything. There might be a link from a piece of text, or from a picture. Website designers try to make it easy for you to spot the links and explain where the link will take you. Also, the **mouse pointer**, which normally looks like this ⌖ will change when you hover it over an object on a web page. If it changes to a little hand like this 🖑 that means that there is a link to another page.

4   Find a hyperlink (any hyperlink) and click on it.

You are now taken to a different web page. This page will probably have lots of information on it, and lots more hyperlinks too.

One of the problems is that you can quite quickly lose track of where you are. After you have clicked on a few hyperlinks, you have lost the page where you started. If this happens:

5   Click the 'Back' button.

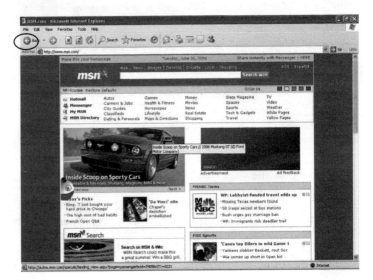

This will take you to the previous page.

6   Click the 'Back' button again.
    This will take you back to the page before that, and so on until eventually you are back where you started.

Another problem is that sometimes when you click on a hyperlink, a new window opens up. This means that your original page is still open in the background. To get back to the original page in this case:

7   Click on the small cross in the top right-hand corner of the window. This window then closes, and your original page is displayed again.

10.3 Structure of web addresses

It is useful to be able to recognize the way that web addresses are put together. Sometimes it will give you a hint about the nature of the site. Most addresses look like this: www.hodder.co.uk

- The www means World Wide Web and most (but not all) addresses start with this. Sometimes you don't even need to type this in.
- The next part tells you the name of the individual or organization who owns the website. In this case it is Hodder (the publisher of this book).
- The last part of the address tells you what type of organization or person owns the website and where it is in the world. The table below shows some common examples.

.com	Stands for 'commercial' and will be a business. Could be anywhere in the world.
.co.uk	This will be a British business.
.org.uk	This will be a British organization, but not a business e.g. a charity.
.gov.uk	This is UK government website.
.ac.uk	This will be a UK college or university. The 'ac' is short for academic.
.au .it .de	These are country codes that appear at the end of an address and indicate which country they come from. There are lots of these. In this example: Australia, Italy and Germany.

10.4 Finding information you need using a search engine

If you do *not* know the web address, you will need to **search** the Internet to find the information you need. To do this, you need a **search engine**.

Search engines are free and you can access them using the Internet. There are lots to choose from but the most common ones are Google™, Yahoo!® and Ask™. They all do the same thing and it is up to you which one you use. The most popular one at the moment is Google™.

A search engine allows you to type in **keywords** that describe what you are looking for. For example, let's say we want to make a donation to the British Red Cross and we need to find the website. You might start by searching for: 'Charities'. It will then search through the web to find web pages that contain information based on the keywords you typed in.

When it has found all the sites, it will display them in a list. The list may take up hundreds of pages.

Hints and tips

Even the best search engine doesn't search every single page on the Internet. You might want to experiment with a couple of different search engines to find the one you like the best. The organizations that provide these search engines are commercial businesses so they will all tell you that theirs is the best.

---

1 Open Internet Explorer®.
2 Type 'www.google.co.uk' into the address bar. The Google™ home page will now load.
3 Type the word 'Charity' into the box as shown in figure on next page top.
4 Click on the button for 'pages from the UK'.

Hints and tips

Clicking the UK button means that you should only get websites based in the UK, although some others may get through.

---

5 Click on the 'Google Search' button.

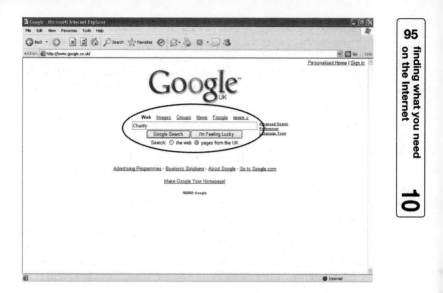

After a few seconds it will show the results pages listing all of the websites that contain information about charities.

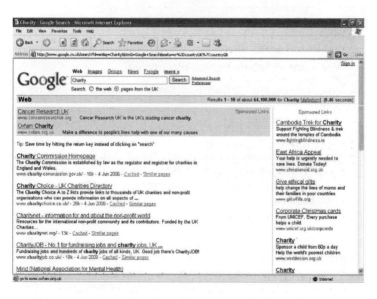

This page contains the first ten websites that contain information that meet your keywords. It also contains some sponsored links, which mean that businesses have paid Google™ so that their websites will appear on this page.

Hints and tips
Each website shown on the results page can be opened by clicking on it. You can read what it says about the website and use this to decide whether it is worth clicking on or not.

In the top right-hand corner you will see how many pages the search engine has found. In this case it has found 64,100,000 pages. This is sometimes called the number of **hits**. It would take years to search through all of these, so we need to narrow down the search.

Let's narrow down the search:

6 Type the words "British Red Cross" into the box. You will find that this reduces the number of hits significantly, and that the website for the British Red Cross is first on the list on the first page of results.

We actually wanted to find out how to donate to the British Red Cross so we could do two things here. We could:

7 Click on the link to the British Red Cross website.
8 Follow the hyperlinks to the donation section.

OR you could refine the search still further:

9 Type the words: "British Red Cross + donation" exactly as shown.

Hints and tips
Putting words inside speech marks means that the search will show only websites that contain those words in that sequence. Using the + sign means that it will only include sites that also contain the word 'donation'.

---

10 Press ENTER. The results page will now show a direct link to the donations web page of the British Red Cross website.

10.5 How to tell whether websites are reliable and trustworthy

Just because a website is listed by a search engine, does not mean that it contains the information you need, or that the information is correct. Anyone can put information onto a website and there are plenty of strange people out there!

It is not always easy to tell how reliable a website is, but there are some general guidelines you can use:

- Rely on websites only if they are from organizations or businesses that you already know and trust.
- Check for an 'About Us' link to see if you can find out who is responsible for the site.
- Check the name of the site. If it is a .gov site for example, you know that it has come from the government (whether you trust it or not is up to you!). If it is .co.uk it could be from anyone.
- Most sites are trying to sell you something, so you need to be as cynical as you would be if confronted with a pushy salesperson in a shop!
- Some websites are what is known as **secure sites**. There is more information on this in Chapter 16.

10.6 Dead links and redirection

Finally, it is quite common to click on a hyperlink and not to get the page you want. This might be for a number of reasons. The web page might no longer exist, or the link might have been set up incorrectly. These are sometimes called **dead links** as they don't take you anywhere. You will most likely get a message on the screen saying that the web page has not been found.

If this happens:

1 Click on 'Back'.
  This will take you back to the page that you linked from. It is worth trying again, as sometimes you just get a bad connection. If you try again and you get the same message, then the link is probably dead and there is nothing you can do about it.

Sometimes you will be redirected to another website. Sometimes this is for genuine reasons, as the website may have been moved to a different address. Sometimes, it is an advertising ploy to take you to a site that then tries to sell you something.

A bit like dead links, all you can do is:

2   Click on 'Back' or click on the cross to close the window.

10.7 Bookmarking websites

When you find a good website, you will probably want to use it over and over again. Rather than having to remember the address, or go through the search engine to find it again, you can add the website to a list of 'favourites'. This is also known as a **bookmark**.

Bookmarking a website means that you can get at it quickly from the menus options. In this example, we will bookmark the Oxfam site:

1   Open Internet Explorer®.
2   Type 'www.oxfam.org.uk' into the address bar and press ENTER.

When the page has opened:

3   Select 'Favorites' from the menu at the top of the screen.
4   Select 'Add Page to Favorites' and click OK.

If you want to go to this site at any time, all you need to do is:

5   Click on 'Favorites' and select the Oxfam website from the list displayed.

Summary

In this chapter we have discussed:

• How to understand and use web addresses
• How to use a search engine
• How to follow hyperlinks and move between web pages
• How to tell whether a website is reliable
• What to do when you get a bad link
• How to bookmark a website

buying products and services online

In this chapter you will learn:

- how to find products and services on the Internet
- how to buy products and services on the Internet
- how to compare prices
- how to add items into your basket
- how to go to an online checkout
- things to watch out for when buying online

Aims of this chapter

This chapter assumes that you have some knowledge of searching the Internet. If this is not the case, it is recommended that you complete Chapter 10 first. This chapter will explain how to search for particular products, compare prices, add items to your basket and then pay for them at the checkout. It also includes some tips on things to look out for when buying online. Examples in this chapter include shopping for electrical items and groceries, but it could equally apply to buying services, such as insurance.

11.1 Introduction

Buying products and services over the **Internet** is pretty much the same as buying them from a shop – you go into the shop, browse, put things in your basket, go to the checkout and pay up. There are a few key differences, which are explained later in the chapter. You might be nervous about buying things **online**, as there is much talk about online fraud. Fraud does happen and you could be a victim, in much the same way as you could be in a normal shop. For specific information on keeping safe online, see Chapter 16.

11.2 Getting started

The first step is to get online and find the products that you want to buy. To do this you either need to:

- Know the Internet address of the **website** that sells the product.
- Use a **search engine** to find a website that sells the product.

There are different approaches to this. You could go to the website of a well-known retailer (e.g. Tesco, PC World) and then **browse** their site to find the product you want. Alternatively, you could type in the name of the product you want (e.g. Samsung DVD player, Hitachi CD player) and see what results you find for them. You could type in more general terms like 'DVD player' which would list all DVD players of all makes.

Another option is the use of comparison sites. These are websites that are set up just to compare the prices of products. They will show you all the places where you can buy the product and list the price that you will be charged.

> **Hints and tips**
> You will remember from Chapter 10 that you need to exercise some caution when using websites and you need to ensure that the site is genuine and reliable.

11.3 Finding the website of a well-known business

Many businesses that have shops also have websites, so your start point might be to find the website of a well-known retailer. For example, Tesco, Asda and Sainsbury's all have websites where you can buy the same products online as you can in the store. Currys and PC World all have online stores where you can order the same products that they have in their stores.

To find these websites:

1 Open Internet Explorer® from the **desktop** or the 'Start' **menu.**
2 When your **home page** is **loaded,** type 'www.google.co.uk' in the **address bar.**
3 When Google™ opens, type 'Asda' in the box and click the 'Search Google' button.
4 As these businesses are so big, their website is almost bound to be the first one in the list.

> **Hints and tips**
> If you don't know the Internet address of a big company, you can just guess at it and you will probably be right. For example, Tesco is www.tesco.com and Asda is www.asda.com

5 Click on the **link** to the website from the Google™ results page. This takes you to the home page of the website from which you can follow the links to different sections.

11.4 Searching for a particular product from a well-known business

If you want to buy a specific product from a specific retailer, for example if you want a Samsung DVD player from Currys, then you should use the **search** function on the Currys website. If you are not fussed which retailer you buy it from, skip to the next section.

Hints and tips

Most big websites have their own search engines that let you search their site. To search the whole of the Internet, you need a search engine such as Google™, Yahoo!® or Ask™.

This example shows how to search for DVD players on the Currys website.

1   In the address bar, type 'www.currys.co.uk'. This is the website of Currys, the electrical retailer.
2   The Currys home page will load and will look something like this although it will have changed since this book was published.

You can now follow the links through the products you are looking for, or use the search engine provided in the website. The links to different sections are listed down the left-hand side in this case. There is a link called 'DVD and Video', which you could click on. Alternatively, you could use the search engine:

3 In the box, type 'Samsung DVD' and click on 'Find'.
The whole of the Currys website will now be searched and the
results will be displayed on a new screen as shown:

In this example, the search engine has found 12 matches with
Samsung DVD and they are listed.
4 **Scroll down** until you find the one you are interested in.
5 Click on the image and you will be taken to a screen that gives
you more information about the product.

On most websites product information usually includes a fairly
detailed specification of the product and some customer reviews.
The customer reviews are often quite useful and are usually
genuine on well-known sites.

11.5 Searching for a product across the whole Internet

There are some real bargains to be had on the Internet. Some
retailers only sell over the Internet, and this gives them a big
advantage over business with shops in that they have lower
overheads in running their business. Often (but not always)
this means that online businesses are cheaper than ones with
shops.

As with normal shopping it is often worth shopping around. To follow through from the example before, if you want a Samsung DVD player and don't care where you buy it from, you would be better searching the whole Internet, rather than just one website.

To do this:

1 Type 'www.google.co.uk' into the address bar in Internet Explorer®.
2 Now type the name of the product into the box and click 'Search Google'.

As you saw in Chapter 10, it is better to be as precise as possible when typing in your search words. If you know you want a Samsung DVD R-130, then type that exactly to narrow down the number of **hits**. If you just want a Samsung DVD player, or just a DVD player of any make, then you should type in the search words accordingly.

3 Type "Samsung DVD R-130" into Google™, click the 'pages from the UK' button and click 'Google Search'.

Hints and tips
Make sure that you click the 'pages from the UK' button or you will get websites from around the world. You can buy products from other countries but they may be liable to higher delivery costs and taxes. Also, it will be difficult to sort out any problems that might occur later.

---

4 You can now start to look through the results and decide which links are worth following. Remember that some links are sponsored which means that businesses have paid the search engine company to put them nearer the top.
5 Click on a few links until you find a site that you trust. You can then complete the purchase online as described later.

11.6 Using a price comparison site

In most cases these days, if you type in a particular product, the first few hits from the search engine will be what are called comparison sites. These websites exist purely to compare the prices of products and services. Most of these are commercial websites that make their money from the suppliers that they recommend and, as such, you need to question how impartial they might be.

They will list all of the suppliers that they know of who sell that product and will show you how much it will cost and provide a link to the supplier's website.

One of the best known is a company called Kelkoo™, which is owned by Yahoo!®

1 Type 'www.kelkoo.co.uk' into the address bar of Internet Explorer®.
2 The Kelkoo™ home page will now load which will look something like this:

Like many sites, it has its own search engine, which you can see near the top of the page.
3 Type 'Samsung DVD' and click the 'Search' button.
All of the Samsung DVD products will now be listed.
4 Locate the product you are interested in and click the 'Compare Prices' button.
A new list is displayed showing all of the websites from which you can buy the product, along with the price. This is a direct comparison of the price of exactly the same product, from all of these different suppliers.

5   Look through the list and choose which supplier you would
    like to use and click on the link.

Hints and tips

Price comparison sites will list some suppliers that you have heard
of and some that you have not. See the general advice in Chapters
10 and 16 about how to identify a legitimate supplier and how to
keep safe when online.

11.7 Making the purchase

After you have found the product you want on a site from which
you want to buy it, it is now time to complete the purchase. Most
sites have a **basket**. This is the same as a basket in a shop i.e. you
put stuff in it. Like a shop you can put things back if you want
to and it is only when you get to the checkout that you must pay
for your items.

Most sites simply have an 'Add to basket' button next to every
product and by clicking it, it puts it into your basket and you
carry on **browsing** for the next item and so on. On some sites it
just says 'add' and on some sites you get a little **icon** (picture) of
a basket.

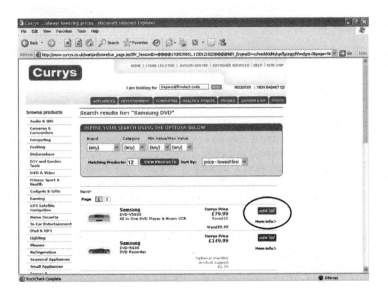

You can view the contents of your basket at any time, and add and remove items from it. All websites look slightly different, but the principle is the same. The Currys basket looks like this:

The 'Remove Item' button does just that, and takes the item out of the basket. The 'Update' button takes you back into the shop so you can put more stuff in your basket and the 'Go to checkout' is what you do when you have finished shopping and want to pay.

1 Click on the 'Go to checkout' option. On other sites, it might simply be called 'Checkout'.

Again, the checkout section of each website will look different but essentially they all the do the same thing. You will be asked for personal details and credit card details. Many sites will ask you to register, which means that they store your details. This can be handy as it means that if you buy anything from them again, they remember all the details from the last time.

2 Complete all of the details that they ask for. This will involve typing in your credit or debit card number. See Chapter 16 for more details on keeping yourself safe online.

> **Hints and tips**
> Filling in the details may take some time as they ask you for quite
> a lot of information. Follow the instructions on the screen. If you
> miss any bits out they will tell you.

The last stage of the checkout process is to confirm the order. At
any point up to here you can simply close the window down and
none of the information you have typed in will be saved.

3   Click 'Confirm'. When you have done this you will usually be
    given the option of printing out an order confirmation. You
    will also receive an order confirmation via email within a few
    minutes.
4   Wait a day or two and the doorbell will ring, and there will
    be your parcel!

11.8 Things to watch out for when buying online

The first point is related to the last one made above and that is,
that you will have to wait for delivery. Many websites will deliver
within a day or two, but some will take longer. Often this is
because they do not have the item in stock, and have to wait for
it. The best advice here is to use websites that are recommended
to you by friends, or that you have used before and know to be
good.

Delivery charges can sometimes be excessive and more than the
actual cost of delivery. Some websites appear to offer cheap products, but then add a large delivery charge. You may not discover
this until quite a long way through the ordering process.
Remember, you can always click on the cross at any time if you
don't like the scale of delivery charges and don't want to proceed.

Watch out for other hidden charges. Some websites charge VAT
on top of the prices that they are quoting on their websites. So
something that looks like a bargain at £99.99 with VAT and
delivery to add on could cost you £137.50. It is the final order
confirmation that must clearly show you what you are paying, so
check this carefully before you confirm the order.

One big disadvantage of the Internet is that you can see only a
picture of what you are buying – you can't see it for real. There
are a couple of things you can do here. The first is a bit cheeky,

but you can pop down to a shop and take a look at it in the flesh and then come home and buy it online. The second is to check whether the website offers a returns policy so that you can get your money back if you don't like the item when it arrives.

11.9 A special note about online grocery shopping

Buying groceries online can be excellent. It can take a long time to go through and select all of the products that you want, but when you have done it once, you can edit the list each week rather than doing it from scratch. You can redeem all of your vouchers as if you were at the supermarket and best of all, someone goes round and gets it all for you.

Some retailers will not charge you extra for this service and some make a small charge. If you live a way from the supermarket this can represent good value as it saves you time and money. However, all retailers do put a limit on how far they will deliver.

Again, ask around among your friends, as some retailers are better than others. For example, do they deliver within the stated time slot, what do they do if the product you want is out of stock, do they select the best fruit and vegetables or the grotty ones off the floor?

Summary

In this chapter we have discussed:
- How to find well-known retailers online
- How to find products online
- How to add items to a basket and go to the checkout
- How to compare prices
- Things to watch out for when buying online
- A few points specific to grocery shopping

12 buying from an online auction

In this chapter you will learn:

- how to set up an eBay™ account
- how to search and browse for products
- how to place a bid
- how to pay for your product
- things to watch out for using eBay™

Aims of this chapter

This chapter will show you how to use the eBay™ auction site. It assumes that you have never used an online auction before and will show you how to register, how to find what you want and how to bid for it, and eventually pay for it. The final section includes some tips on buying successfully from eBay™.

12.1 Introduction

eBay™ is currently the world's biggest **online** auction site boasting more than 180 million users worldwide with at least 3 million items for sale at any one time.

It works much in the same way as a traditional auction in that items are offered for sale, you look at them and read the description, and then decide whether you want to bid on the item or not. Many other people will be doing the same thing and bidding against you. The big difference with a real auction is the period of time over which the bidding takes place, as it can be several days. At the end of this period, if your bid is the highest, you win. You then pay for the product and the seller sends it to you, or you go and pick it up.

Although eBay™ was originally intended for items of relatively low value, it is now possible to buy virtually anything on eBay™ including cars, holidays and even houses.

12.2 Getting started

First, you need to register. To do this, you *must* already have an email address. If you do not have one, refer to Chapter 8.

1 Open Internet Explorer® either from the **desktop** or from the 'Start' **menu**.
2 In the **address bar**, type 'www.ebay.co.uk'

Hints and tips
eBay™ operates in more than 30 countries, so make sure that you use the correct version for the country that you are in.

The opening page is displayed and will look something like this.

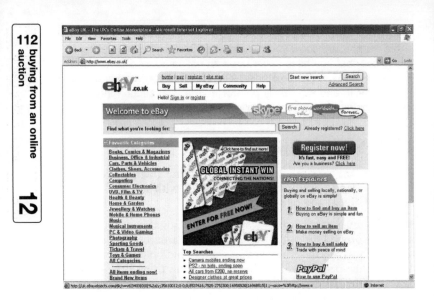

3   Click on the 'Register now!' button.

You now have to fill in a form (something you will be getting used to by now when using the **Internet**). This will ask you for your personal details and email contact details. You will also be asked to think of a **user ID** and **password,** which you will need to use every time you **log on** to eBay™.

4   Complete the form. This may take a few minutes.
5   Make a note of your user ID and remember your password.
6   When you have completed the form, you will be sent an email from eBay™. This is an automatic process and should be instant.
7   Go to your **email account** and open the email from eBay™.
8   In the email, you are asked to click on a **link** that will activate your eBay™ account. Click on the link.

It will take you back to the eBay™ **website** where you can now start bidding for products.

To make sure you are in the 'Buy' section, click on the link to 'Buy' in the top left-hand corner of the page:

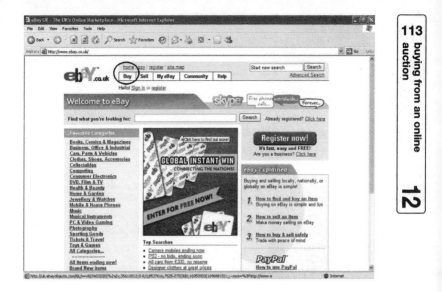

12.3 Finding what you want

There are two ways to find the items you are looking for:

- You can **browse**, which means you can look through a wide range of products under certain categories.
- You can **search**, which means you type in a few **keywords** that describe the item you want and it will search through all the items and display only those items that match the description you have typed in.

Browsing for an item

If you do not specifically know what you want, then browsing is the best option. For example, if you want to look at antique chairs, but do not have a specific items in mind:

1   Look through the categories until you find the one you want. In this case, it will be under 'Antiques and Art' so click on this link.

You are now presented with a more detailed list of categories within the Antiques and Art section.

2   Under Antique Furniture click on 'Chairs'.

You are now at the screen that lists all of the items that are for sale under this category. In this example, there are 1172 items for sale.

3 To view the entire list of items for sale, you need to **scroll down**. It is not possible to show all 1172 items on one page, so at the bottom of the first page, there are links to several other pages.

On the left-hand side of each page, you will see that there are further subcategories. In this case, there are categories for 'Victorian', 'Pre-Victorian', etc. This will help you to narrow down your search reducing the number of items listed.

Hints and tips

It would take you hours to view all 1172 items in this example so it would be better to try to narrow down the search if you can using the subcategories.

Searching for an item

The preferred method of finding what you want on eBay™ is to type in a few keywords that describe it. As you saw in the previous section, browsing through categories can be time-consuming as there are often so many items for sale.

1 Click on the 'Buy' button again to take you back to the main buying page where all the categories are listed.

At the top of this page, there is a 'Search' box. This example will show you how to search for a specific item, a garden hammock.

2 Click in the 'Search' box and type: Garden hammock.

You can narrow down the search by searching only within a category using the box to the right of the search box.

3 In the 'In this category' box, which currently reads 'All categories', select 'Home & Garden'.

Hints and tips
If you do not know which category something fits in to, you can just leave this box set to 'All categories'.

---

4 Click on 'Search'.

After a few seconds, you will be presented with a list of all the garden hammocks that are currently for sale.

12.4 Selecting your item

Once you have located an item that you are interested in, you need to get a few more details about it and the seller. In the first instance you need to know the price, how many bids there are on it, and how long there is left on the auction.

The screen listing all of the items gives you some useful information to help you decide whether to look in more detail at the item.

These are:

Photograph of the product – the seller puts this on. If there isn't a photograph, be suspicious.
Item Title – a brief description put on by the seller.
Bids – shows you the number of people who have put in a bid on this item. If it is displaying the 'Buy It Now' symbol it means that you must pay the price quoted, you cannot bid for it.
Price – the highest price currently bid.
Postage – how much the seller will charge you to send the item. Keep an eye out for over-the-top charges.
PayPal – a method of online payment where you pay for the item via email using a credit/debit card. This can make the transaction easier as you don't have to wait for cheques to clear.
Time Left – how many days or hours there are left until the auction closes. When the auction closes, the highest bidder at that point wins.

This information is displayed for every item that is for sale. If you are still interested in the item you can now find out more about it and the seller.

12.5 Finding out more about the items and the seller

To view more details about any specific item:

Click on the photograph or on the item title.

This then displays a further page that gives you details about the product, usually some more photographs and the seller rating, which gives you an idea of how reliable the seller is.

A fuller description of the product can be obtained by scrolling down the page.

On the right-hand side is a seller rating. When people buy items from eBay™ they are asked to rate the seller and make comments about them. You can view these comments and read the ratings by following these links. It will show you the number of people who have commented and provide an overall rating. In this example, the seller has 74 comments and they are all positive giving a 100% rating.

You can contact the seller direct to ask them questions about the product or delivery arrangements, etc. This is advisable on larger value items in particular.

> **Hints and tips**
> eBay™ provides useful hints and tips about trading on their website. For example, this page in the diagram above has a link to a section on safe buying tips.

12.6 Making a bid

Once you have found the item you want, you can bid on it. If there is a 'Buy It Now' option, you can just buy it at this point without having to bid at all. Assuming that bidding is required:

1 From the current screen, click on the 'Place Bid' button.
2 This will take you to a screen where you can type in how much you want to bid.

A useful feature here is that you can type in the maximum amount you are prepared to pay and eBay™ will automatically keep increasing your bid, if you are out-bid by someone else. If the price goes beyond your maximum bid, it will stop bidding and you will not win the auction.

3 Finally, you are asked to confirm the bid. It is at this point that you are entering a legal contract to buy the item. So if you win, you must buy it. Only click on 'Confirm Bid' if you want to buy the item!

4 The next step is to keep an eye on the bidding from time to time, or just wait until the time runs out and see whether you have won.

eBay™ has a feature called 'My eBay'. You can opt to 'Watch this item', which means that it will put the item you are interested in into a list for you, where you can watch the progress of the bidding.

To do this, from the item's description screen like the one shown, click on 'Watch this item'.

5 To view the 'My eBay' area, click on 'My eBay' near the top of the screen. The My eBay screen looks like this screen on next page. The hammock is listed here and it is possible to view the bidding as it progresses.

12.7 Winning and paying

When you win an auction for an item or if you opt to 'Buy It Now' you need to pay for the item. If you win or lose an auction, you will be informed by email. There are different ways of paying. You are supplied with contact details of the seller. This is often just an email address or maybe a phone number. If this is the case, you could just contact the seller and make arrangements like any other buying/selling arrangement.

Alternatively, you can do it all online or via the post with no need for any contact at all. Many sellers accept cheques but will require you to post the cheque and allow time for it to clear. This is where the seller rating is important, as you need to be confident that you will receive the item.

The other option is **PayPal**. This is a free and **secure service** where you pay using your credit or debit card via email. This is quicker than a cheque as the money will transfer much more quickly. It also provides protection in the eventuality that the item is not sent, or that it is significantly different from the way it was described.

To use PayPal you will need to register with the PayPal website first. This process is similar to registering for eBay™ in the first place and can be done by following the links to PayPal from the eBay™ site or by typing 'www.paypal.co.uk' into the address bar and then clicking on the 'Sign Up Now' link.

Once you have done this you will be able to use this method wherever the seller accepts PayPal. You will receive an email confirming your order, and you click on the 'Pay Now' option.

12.8 Things to watch out for using eBay™

In common with anything else on the Internet, there are plenty of dodgy people out there who might try to rip you off. The anonymous nature of the Internet perhaps makes this a bit easier for these people. The best advice is to use the seller ratings to make a judgement about how reliable someone might be.

Decide how much you want to spend and stick to it. In common with traditional auctions, it can be tempting to keep upping the price that you are willing to pay, only to regret it later. Many bidders leave it until the last minute to make their bids; so don't get caught up in a bidding war.

Make sure you are aware of all the charges that will be added. Keep an eye on postage costs and VAT. Many businesses now use eBay™ as their main way of selling products, and they will have to add on VAT. Also, make sure that the item is for sale in your country, or you may have to pay additional shipping costs and tax.

Finally, eBay™ has become an international phenomenon and as a result, there is a lot of information written about it. A good starting point is the company's own Help centre, which can be accessed by clicking the 'Help' tab on their **home page**.

Summary

In this chapter we have discussed:
- How to register with eBay™
- How to browse and search for items
- How to make a bid
- How to make a payment
- Things to watch out for using eBay™

13

communicating with other people using the Internet

In this chapter you will learn:

- how to use the Internet to keep in touch
- how to use chat rooms
- how to access newsgroups
- how to make phone calls over the Internet
- how to make video calls over the Internet

Aims of this chapter

In Chapter 8, you were introduced to email, which is just one way in which you can communicate with people over the Internet. This chapter will show you other methods of communicating with people who you know, and with other people who you don't know but may share the same interests as you. It covers chat rooms, newsgroups and Internet phone calls. It uses common examples of websites that offer these services although others are available.

13.1 Introduction

When your computer is connected to the **Internet,** you are part of a massive collection of computers all communicating with each other. It is possible to communicate using text, voice and video with anybody who is connected.

There are several ways of doing this, some of which require special **software,** most of which is free from the Internet. However, to access most of these efficiently, you will need a **broadband** connection, otherwise the connection may be too slow.

13.2 Chat rooms

An Internet **chat room** is a 'virtual' room where people can enter and talk about anything they like. Chat rooms normally have a specific theme, for example you might enter a chat room to discuss politics, or the news, or computers. There are hundreds of chat rooms to choose from on the Internet.

This example will look at the chat rooms provided by Yahoo!®, which is a well-known and well-respected Internet business.

Hints and tips

There are lots of dodgy chat rooms out there. Only use chat rooms from well-known and reliable websites.

1 Open Internet Explorer® either from the **desktop** or the Start **menu.**
2 In the **address bar,** type 'chat.yahoo.com'

Hints and tips
Notice that it was not necessary to type in the www for the Yahoo!®
web address.

The Yahoo!® chat page is now displayed.

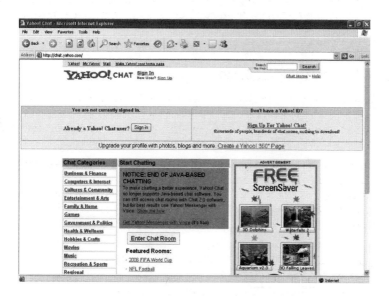

You can see some of the 'Chat Categories' that are available.
Before you enter a room you will have to register, which
means filling in another form:

3 Click on 'Sign Up For Yahoo! Chat'. You will now be presented with a form to fill in, which will look a bit like the
picture on next page. This may take some time to fill in. You
will only have to do it once as next time you **log in,** you can
use the details that you are about to set up.
4 Click in each box and type in the details. You will be asked
to invent a **user name** for yourself and a **password.** Make this
something that is easy to remember.

Hints and tips
You don't have to disclose personal information if you don't want
to.

5 Click the 'I Agree' button at the bottom when you have finished. If you have made any mistakes or missed anything, you will be asked to complete those bits again.

Hints and tips

Every time you fill in a form on the Internet there is a chance that it will lead to you getting emails from these people. Just so you know.

---

6 Click on 'Continue to Yahoo Chat'.
7 You can now choose which category of chat room you want to enter. For this example, select 'Family & Home'.
8 A long list of different chat rooms will now be displayed. The number of people in each room is shown to help you decide whether to enter that room or not. Select 'Genealogy' and click on the first chat room available.
   The chat room will now open, which may take a few seconds (see picture on top of next page).
9 When the room has connected, click 'Continue' and then click 'Start Chat Now'.

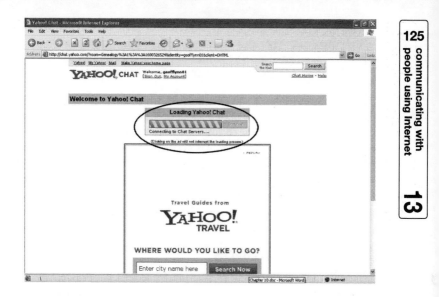

You are now in the chat room. The names of all the people in the room are listed on the right. The main screen will display what they are typing in.

10 Type your comment into the box at the bottom and click 'Send'.

11 The other people in the chat room will now (hopefully) respond to your comments and questions and you can start chatting.
12 When you have finished, just click on the cross in the top right-hand corner.

There are hundreds of chat rooms available and some are better than others. Yahoo!® regulates its chat rooms to get rid of undesirable people. Some chat rooms don't. You need to exercise some caution here. Many well-known **websites** have a 'chat' option, which will work in a way similar to the Yahoo!® chat rooms.

Another factor is that some websites are specific to one country while others are global. You might find yourself in a chat room, therefore, where you do not speak the language.

13.3 Newsgroups

A **newsgroup** is an **online** notice board where people can post messages and respond to messages that others have posted. It is a bit like a chat room, but it is not live. There are literally thousands of different newsgroups on the go at any time covering every imaginable topic.

As with everything else on the Internet, you can access newsgroups in a number of different ways. In this example, Yahoo!® newsgroups will be used.

1 Open Internet Explorer® and type 'groups.yahoo.com' into the address bar.
2 This will load the Yahoo!® Groups page.
3 You can log on to this using the same **user ID** that you created to use the Yahoo!® chat room.
4 Once you have logged in, you can now search for a group on a specific topic, or click on one of the categories listed (see picture on next page).
5 Once you have found the newsgroup you want, you will have to register with the group.
6 After this you will see all of the messages that have been posted and the name of the person who posted it. The idea now is that you respond to the message and a **thread** develops, which is an ongoing list of messages and responses.
7 To read a message, click on it.
8 To respond to a message, go to the bottom of the message and click on the 'Reply' button, and type in your message and click 'Send'.

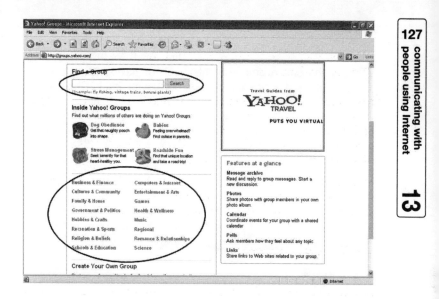

As with chat rooms, some well-known websites also have a
'notice board' or 'forum' option, which is effectively the same
thing.

9 Click on the cross when complete.

13.4 Phone calls

There is a new way of communicating over the Internet called
VOIP, which stands for Voice Over Internet Protocol. This
means that you can talk into your computer to someone else on
his or her computer. If you have a web cam, it is also possible to
see the person you are talking to and for them to see you (this is
covered in the next section). This service is free.

For this to work, you do need a broadband Internet connection,
a web cam (which usually has a microphone built into it) and
some speakers. You may need to go back to Chapter 2 to find out
how to add these to your **computer system** if you do not have
them already.

There are different websites where you can **download** VOIP. This
section will be using a popular one called Skype™.

First, you will need to download the Skype™ software onto your
computer. You will also need to have someone with a computer

and Skype™ at the other end so you have got someone to talk to.

> This is the first example in this book of having to download software from the Internet. We first discussed this in Chapter 5.

1 Open Internet Explorer®.
2 Type 'www.skype.com' into the address bar. The Skype™ **home page** will now open.
3 Click on the **links** to 'download' until the software starts to download. You will see a screen that looks like this:

It may take a few minutes to download the software.

When the download is complete:

4 Click 'Run'.
5 Another screen will now be displayed. You will need to click to accept the terms of the licence and then click 'OK'. The main Skype™ screen will now be displayed. As with chat rooms and newsgroups you must first register, which means choosing a name and password.

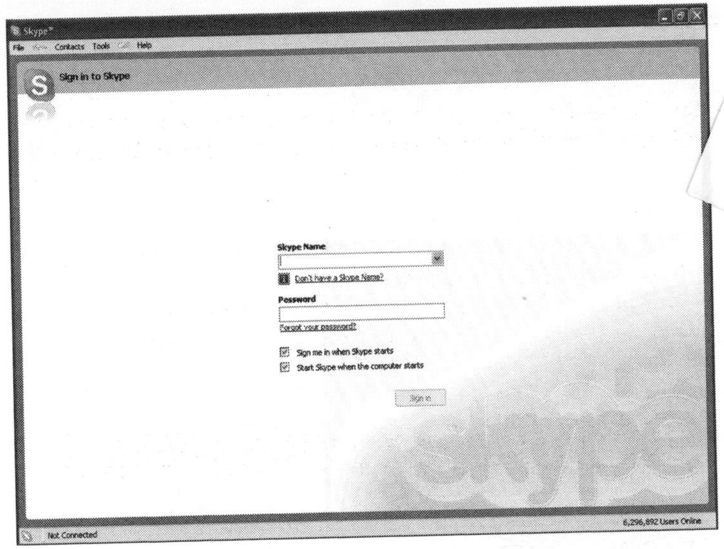

6 Complete the form making a note of the 'Skype Name' that you have chosen.

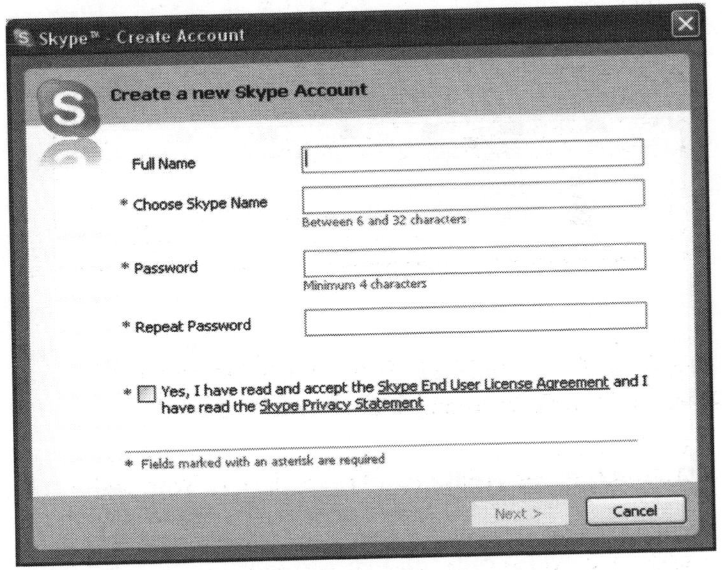

7 Click on 'Next' and proceed to use Skype™.
  The following screen is displayed:

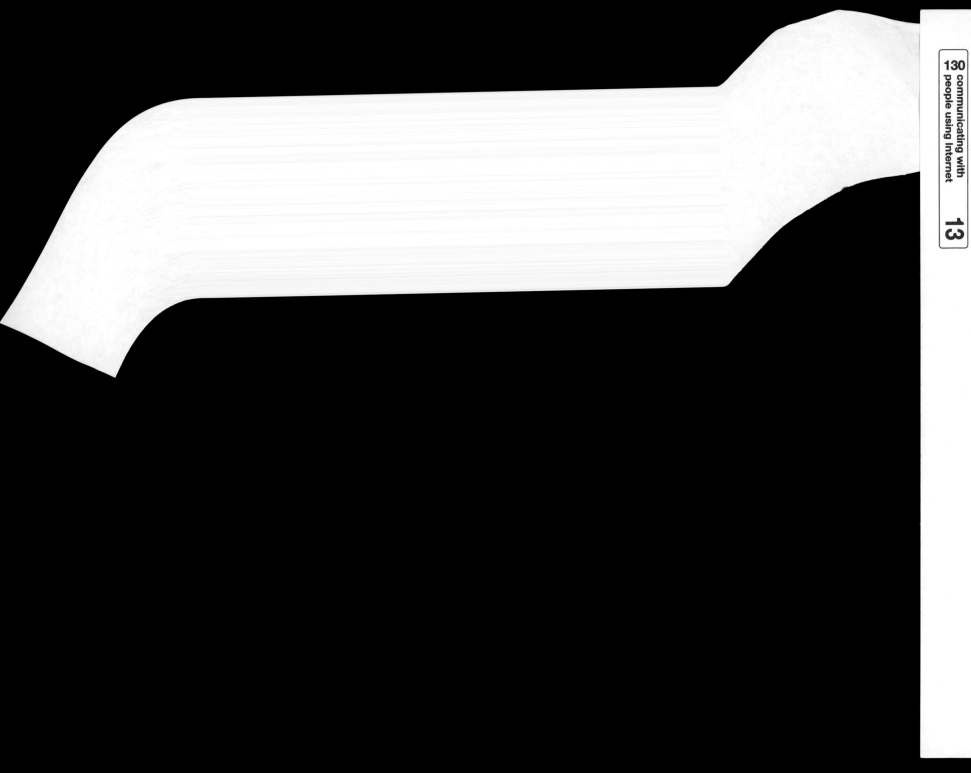

This is the part where you need someone to call and you need
to know their Skype Address.

8 Click on the 'Add Contact' button in the top left-hand
corner.

9 Type in the Skype Name of the person you want to contact.

10 Now click on the 'Contacts' tab and double click on this
person's Skype Name.

11 The software will then dial that person as if you were on the
phone.

12 If they are online, they will answer and you will hear their
voice coming out of your speakers. You can now talk to them
as if it were a normal phone call.

13 To end the call, click on the red phone symbol at the bottom.

If someone calls you using Skype™, you will hear your computer
ringing and you will need to click on the green phone symbol to
accept the call.

13.5 Video calls

Once you have established a voice connection, you will be given
the option to video call with that person if you both have web
cams set up on your computer.

Click on the video option and you will be seen as well as heard.

If you have a webcam and the person that you are calling has a webcam, you should automatically be able see them on the screen. They will be able to see you too. If you cannot see them, or they cannot see you:

1 Select 'Tools' from the menu across the top.
2 Select 'Options'.
3 Select 'Video' from the list of options on the left-hand side.
4 Make sure the 'Enable Skype Video' box is ticked.
5 Make sure the 'Start my video automatically' box is ticked.
6 Click 'Save'.
7 You should now be able to see the person you are talking to.

Hints and tips

Sending and receiving video images and sound requires broadband Internet speeds. Even with broadband, the sound may break up a bit, or the images may be jerky.

Summary

In this chapter we have discussed:
• How to access chat rooms
• How to access newsgroups
• How to make phone calls and video calls over the Internet

14

accessing music, film, radio and TV over the Internet

In this chapter you will learn:

- the basics of accessing music, film, radio and TV using the Internet
- the software needed to get access to music and TV called 'players'
- the difference between legal and illegal content
- the difference between 'live' and 'download' services
- how to download music and film

> **Aims of this chapter**
> This chapter will start you on the road to understanding how to access music, film and TV using your Internet connection. It will focus on the legal sites where these materials can be accessed, explaining what software is required to get at it, and how to store it on your computer for later use.

14.1 Introduction

Multimedia material (that's sound, images and text) is what the **Internet** is all about. Over recent years there has been a massive increase in the use of the Internet for viewing and listening to films, TV programmes, radio stations and music in general. The growth in the use of multimedia is because more and more people now have **broadband** Internet access, which means that it is accessible much more quickly than before.

> **Hints and tips**
> If you do not have broadband Internet access, you will find accessing music and film very slow indeed.

There is a mixture of things on offer. You can view TV programmes and listen to live radio. You can **download** music and films, which means that you save it onto your own computer so you can watch/listen again and again. There are two problems:

- There is so much of it about at the moment that it is often hard to find what you want.
- A lot of the material on offer is illegal because the **websites** offering it do not own the copyright.

14.2 Getting started

If you want to listen to or view multimedia content then you will need a piece of **software** called a **player** or **media player**. There are lots of different players to choose from. Some of them are free. Two common ones are called Windows Media® Player, which you will probably already have, and one called RealPlayer™, which you can download from the Internet. All players basically work in the same way – they let you play sounds and movies.

This chapter assumes that Windows Media® Player is already **installed**.

You will also need a pair of speakers plugged into your computer. Most computers have an internal speaker, but this is very quiet, so it is recommended that you get some external speakers. You will also need a broadband Internet connection.

Hints and tips
You can install either Windows Media® Player or RealPlayer™ from the BBC website for free (www.bbc.co.uk).

14.3 Listening to live radio

A Google™ **search** will show you that there are hundreds of live radio stations available over the Internet. Some a free and some are paid-for services. Some of these will be better than others. This section will show you how to access the BBC radio stations.

1 Open Internet Explorer® from the **desktop** or the Start **menu**.
2 In the **address bar**, type www.bbc.co.uk/radio
   This is the **home page** for the radio section of the BBC website. All of the radio stations are listed on this page, with links that allow you to listen live to each station. For example, to listen to Five Live:
3 Find the **link** to Five Live and click on it.

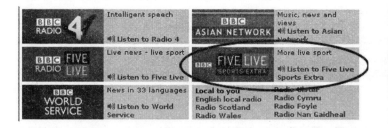

After a few seconds, the media player software will open and it will start to play. Make sure your speakers are switched on at this point! The media player will be shown in a new window (see picture on next page top).

If you do not have a media player set up, it will tell you at this point and give you the option of downloading it now.

You can now **minimize** this window and continue listening to the radio while you carry on doing other things on your computer.

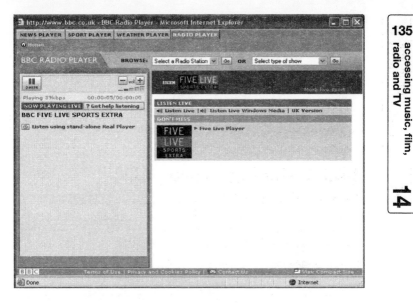

To stop listening:

4   Click on the cross to close the window. A message will ask
    you if you are sure, click 'Yes'.

14.4 Watching TV programmes

Like the radio stations, you will also find that there are hundreds of
TV stations available on the Internet. Again, some of these will be
truly awful and some might be worth tuning in to. Some websites
will allow you to watch for free while others make a charge. Often,
you will get snippets of programmes for free and you have to pay
for the whole programme. Some stations, like the BBC, will allow
you to watch whole programmes for free but only for a limited time.

The media player used to listen to radio is also used to watch TV
and movies. The media player software knows automatically
whether it is radio or movie and will display it accordingly.

This section will show you how to access TV programmes available on the BBC website.

1   Open Internet Explorer® from the desktop or the Start menu.
2   In the address bar, type www.bbc.co.uk/tv
    This is the home page for the TV section of the BBC website.
    It contains links to the various BBC channels. Unlike the

radio, you cannot view all of the programmes live, but there are many available. For example, to view News 24:

3   Click on the link to 'News 24'.
4   Click on the link to 'Watch' news in video. After a few seconds, the player software will **load** automatically in a new window and you will be able to watch the news.

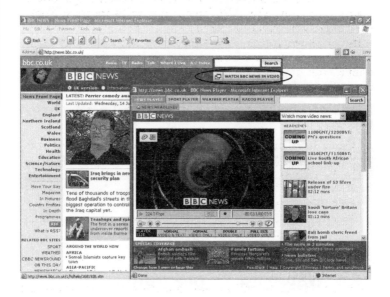

5   To close, simply click on the cross in the top right-hand corner of the window.

14.5 Downloading music and film

Downloading is the process of saving files from the Internet onto your own computer so that you can use them again and again. With the radio and TV that you have viewed, you have to be on the BBC website to be able to do it. If you download music and video, you have the **file** that contains it on your computer and you can load it at any time.

There is an awful lot of music and film available on the Internet. As with anything else on the Internet, a lot of it is rubbish and a lot of it may not be legal. Legal download sites will charge you for downloading files, illegal ones will not.

There are genuine free downloads available but unfortunately there is no way of telling whether sites are genuine or not. As a rule, if it's free and it's on a website that you have never heard of, it is probably illegal. To be on the safe side, you should always pay for your downloads unless they are from a well-known site.

This section will show you how to access a genuine legal download service using **iTunes™**. This is free software from Apple, the people who make the **iPod™** music player. The iTunes™ software allows you to **browse** for music and video of different genre (it's not all pop music) and then download and pay for it **online**. You do *not* have to have an iPod™ to be able to use iTunes™.

If you do not already have the iTunes™ software you will need to download it:

1 Open Internet Explorer® from the desktop or the Start menu.
2 In the address bar, type www.apple.com
3 Follow the link to 'iPod' and 'iTunes'.
4 Follow the link to 'Download iTunes'.
5 You will need to type in your email address and then click the 'Download' button.

Hints and tips
This is quite a big file and will take several minutes to download. If you have an iPod™, this software will be in the box on a CD so it would be quicker to use that.

Once the iTunes™ software is downloaded:

1 Open the iTunes™ software either by double clicking on the **icon** from the desktop or selecting it from the Start menu.
2 The software will then open (see picture on next page top)
3 Make sure that the 'Music Store' is selected by clicking on it on the left-hand side.
   From here you can access a range of downloads including music, movies, and audio books. It will load up the pop music pages, which you may or may not want.
4 To select different music types, select the 'Choose Genre' option and select what you want from the list.
5 You can now browse through the site. This is exactly the same as the online shopping that you did in Chapter 11.

Once you have found what you want you can click on the option
to buy it. As with all online purchases you will have to register
your details and type in your credit or debit card details.

When you buy a movie or album it will then be sent direct over
the Internet and you will be able to access it in the iTunes™ software. To do this:

1   Click on 'Library' on the left-hand side of the iTunes™ soft-
    ware. This will list all of your downloads. To play them:
2   Find the one you want and double click on it. It will then start
    to play.

14.6 Other download websites

There are many websites to choose from and they change daily.
iTunes™ is one option. Whichever one you choose they all work
in a similar way, although it may take a while to find the options.

In this chapter, you have used Windows Media® Player and we
have mentioned RealPlayer™, which are two of the most
common. Both of these have links in their software to online
stores where you can buy music and video. The advantage of
using iTunes™, Windows Media® Player or RealPlayer™ is that
you can be sure that they are legal sites.

14.7 Common features of media player software

All media players allow you to select which files you want to play, be it music or film. They all have controls on them that allow you to control the file being played. These are similar to the controls you would get on a real CD or DVD player. They allow you to Play, Pause, Rewind, Fast Forward and Stop.

Luckily, there are standard symbols for these controls. This diagram shows the symbols from Windows Media® Player.

Play/Pause Stop Rewind Fast Forward Sound on/off Volume

You can stop the file playing at any time and close the software, by clicking on the cross in the top right-hand corner of the window.

Summary

In this chapter we have discussed:

- How to listen to live radio on the Internet
- How to watch TV on the Internet
- How to download music and film
- How to use a media player
- The difference between legal and illegal downloading

15
other common uses of the Internet

In this chapter you will learn:

- further common uses of the Internet including: how to do your banking online; how to book a holiday; how to find transport information; how to get access to government information; how to get access to local information; how to trace your family tree

> **Aim of this chapter**
> The aim of this chapter is to give you some ideas about the various things you can use the Internet for. It is not intended to give you step-by-step guidance on everything that the Internet can be used for, as that would need several books! Rather, it is to give you a taster of some of the uses you could put it to.

15.1 Introduction

Once you start to use the **Internet** you realize that there are only a few basic skills that you need to get to grips with. For example:

- using a **search engine** such as Google™
- **scrolling** through **web pages**
- finding and clicking on **links**
- using the forward and back buttons
- filling in **online** forms

Once you have done these few things, the world (wide web) is your oyster.

The content of the Internet is changing continually. New **websites** are created, are changed, or deleted all the time. New Internet crazes come and go. At the time of writing, for example, **blogging** is very popular. A blog is a web log, or diary. People keep these online and let other people read them. If you want to find out more about it, then just type blog into an Internet search engine and off you go. In fact, if you want to find out about anything, just type it into a search engine and off you go.

In Chapters 10 to 14, you looked at how the Internet could be used for online shopping, using auction sites and communicating with others. Other common uses are listed below.

15.2 Online banking

Online banking has become increasingly popular in recent years. You can do virtually everything that you can do in a normal bank with the exception of paying real money and cheques in, and getting real money out. You can view your accounts, transfer money, pay bills, set up direct debits and standing orders, and view statements. You have access to your bank at all times.

All of the major banks offer an online services, so you can still use your branch or post office for certain transactions if you want to. Some banks are only Internet based.

Security is a serious consideration so you are advised to read the guidance notes on how to keep your personal information safe in Chapter 16, and to deal only with a reputable and well-known bank.

You will have to complete an online registration form and in order to access your account, every time you **log on** you will be asked for the sort code, account number, a security code, and a secret question to make it virtually impossible for anyone else to get into your account.

15.3 Booking holidays

The process of booking a holiday is the same as any other online purchase. You find the one you want, complete the form online and make a payment online using a credit card. There are some bargains to be had from buying online.

All of the same advice applies here as with any other online purchase. Make sure you know whom you are dealing with (all major travel agents have websites as well as shops) and make sure that the payment is made securely.

15.4 Transport information

You can use the Internet to check train times and book tickets, or for maps and directions, or even to get up-to-date traffic information.

For train times and tickets, try www.nationalrail.co.uk or www.thetrainline.com Both are private companies. Both websites are owned by different groups of train and transport companies and both offer a similar service. You type in where you want to go and when and a search engine goes off and **searches** its database and comes back with the details of the departure and arrival times and the routes. You can also buy your ticket online.

For road information, you can try www.theaa.com or www.rac.co.uk Both have a free route-planning feature, which allows you to type in where you are departing from and where you want to go to. You can do this using place names or postcodes. It will then produce a map and a detailed route, both of which you can print out and take with you. Both sites also have up-to-date traffic reports.

If you just want a map, then try www.multimap.co.uk which has online maps. You type in a location and it will show you a map of the area. You can zoom in and out of the map as required.

15.5 Government information

The government has policies about providing access to public information. Much of it is now available online. Government websites are identified by the .gov at the end of the address.

A good place to start is www.direct.gov.uk This is what is called a **portal** site, which means that it is a central point that links lots of other websites together. So in theory, from this site, you can access all of the government websites and web pages of which there are thousands and thousands (see picture on next page top).

You can now either follow the various **hyperlinks** from this page, or use the search box in the top right-hand corner. For example, to find information on pensions:

1 Type 'Pensions' into the search box and click 'Go'.

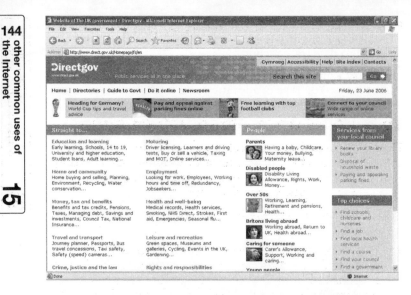

A list of all pages relating to pensions is now displayed. This is a bit like a results page that Google™ would produce.

2 Scan through and click on the links that you think are relevant to what you want to find.

3   If the page you have linked to does not give you what you need, click 'Back' and try another link.

You can also do things like pay for your TV licence (www. tvlicensing.co.uk) or car tax (www.direct.gov.uk/taxdisc).

15.6 Local government information

There is an abundance of local government information available. This is usually provided through websites maintained by your county council. Each county council will have its own website, so the easiest way to find it is:

Type, for example, "Lincolnshire County Council" into a search engine.

The use of the double speech marks in a search engine means that it will find websites with references to those words, in that order. So instead of finding any website with any reference to Lincolnshire or County or Council, it will find websites with reference to Lincolnshire County Council. Type in your council name like this and it will come up first in the list of results.

You can now follow the links to find what you are interested in or by using the search box in the top right-hand corner.

15.7 Tracing your family tree

There is a lot of information now available that will help you if you are trying to trace your family tree. Information and services are offered by government websites, some not-for-profit groups and organizations, and of course, lots of commercial websites that will charge you for their services.

- A good place to start is www.nationalarchives.gov.uk/census This provides links to all of the censuses that are currently available and provides links to useful advice about tracing your family tree.
- There are several genealogy websites run by not-for-profit organizations online. Try www.genuki.org.uk or www.silver surfers.net/interests-genealogy for information and links.
- The BBC also provides a family history section on their website at www.bbc.co.uk/history/familyhistory which provides information, advice and links.

Also bear in mind that you will find plenty of forums and **chat rooms** with a genealogy theme, which you can use and communicate with other people who will be able to pass on hints and tips.

Summary
In this chapter we have discussed:
- Common uses of the Internet including: online banking; booking a holiday; accessing transport information; accessing national and local government information; tracing your family tree

16

keeping safe online

In this chapter you will learn:

- what risks are involved when using the Internet: identity theft; viruses and worms; hacking; undesirable material; premium diallers
- how you can protect yourself against these risks
- advice on buying online
- advice on passwords

Aim of this chapter

The aim of this chapter is to give some advice on what threats and risks there are on the Internet (e.g. fraud, identity theft and viruses) and how you can take steps to minimize or prevent any problems that might arise. There is a range of threats and the purpose of this chapter is to make you aware of them. This chapter should be seen as a basic introduction to a large and ever-changing problem so it is recommended that you ask your computer supplier about how they can help you with some of these things.

16.1 Introduction

The **Internet** is a global connection of computers with the connections being made by telephone cables and satellites. It all works like the telephone system and **logging on** to the Internet is a bit like making a telephone call. In fact, your computer has its own number (called an **IP address**), which is transmitted whenever you are **online**.

The Internet is unregulated in this country, and pretty much anyone can get access to it. Unfortunately this means that it is open to abuse. This chapter lists the threats that exist and, in each case, explains what you can do about them.

16.2 Identity theft

Identify theft occurs when someone obtains personal information about you which means that they can pretend to be you, usually for fraudulent reasons. They could buy things from the Internet in your name, or perhaps borrow money or even clear out your bank account.

There are a number of ways that they can obtain the information:

Phishing – this is where someone sends you an email claiming to be from your bank. They will ask for personal information, or direct you to a fake **website** that asks you for personal information. These emails can look very convincing.

What to do about it:

- Banks will never email you to ask you for personal information such as PIN codes and passwords. If you are asked for it, don't give it.

- Make sure that when you are doing any banking over the Internet that the site is secure. **Secure sites** have https in the address or display a small padlock in the bottom right-hand corner of the screen.

This is the log-on page for the Co-operative Bank. Notice how the address has the https at the beginning and there is a padlock icon. Do not disclose any personal information unless the site has both of these showing.

Spyware/Adware – this is **software** that installs itself on your computer without you knowing about it. It can do this any time you are on the Internet. It can collect personal information that you fill in when online.

What to do about it:

- You can **download** free software from the Internet that will check your computer for spyware, or you can buy software that will do it for you. This type of software is called spyware removal software.
- Keep your version of Windows® XP up to date. Once you have bought Windows® XP you are entitled to free **updates** from their website (www.microsoft.com).

16.3 Viruses and worms

Viruses and **worms** are software that install themselves on your computer without you knowing about it. This normally happens when you download something from the Internet or when you open an email. Like human viruses, a computer virus or worm will infect your computer causing all sorts of problems. Some are worse than others. Really bad ones will delete everything on your computer.

What to do about it:

- Download only from reputable sites or secure sites as explained above.
- Do not open emails (especially email **attachments**) if you do not know who they are from.
- Delete any **spam** emails immediately and do not open them.
- Use **anti-virus software**. You can get free software from the Internet or you can buy it from companies such as McAfee or Norton.
- Keep your anti-virus software up to date as new viruses come out every day.
- Keep your version of Windows® XP up to date as many updates contain fixes for well-known viruses.

16.4 Hacking

Hacking is when someone gains unauthorized access to your computer. They can do this any time you are connected to the Internet. You will not even know that it is happening. Hackers do it for various reasons. Often it is just bored teenagers, but some hackers do it with the intention of getting your personal information.

What to do about it:

- Install a **firewall**. This is software and **hardware** that examines information that is being passed to your computer while you are online. If it finds something it doesn't like, it will block it. If you are using Windows® XP you will already have a fire-wall.
- Turn off the Internet. Only stay online (connected to the Internet) if you need to be. At other times, log yourself off. To do this:

1 Click on 'Start', and then 'Connect to'.

2 Click on 'All Connections'.
   You will be shown any connections that are currently being made between you and the outside world. It will look like this.

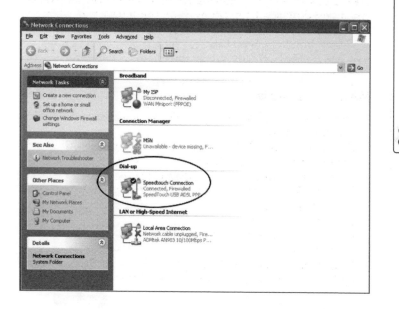

This computer has four connections but only one of them is actually connected. To disconnect:
3 Right click any connection that is connected and select 'Disconnect'.

16.5 Undesirable material

The unregulated nature of the Internet means that you can get access to plenty of undesirable material. Often you will click on a site that you think is perfectly innocent only to find that it contains undesirable content. This may be of particular concern if children have access to your computer.

What to do about it:

• Use your common sense. If you don't like what you see, click on the cross immediately to close the website.
• Install **filtering or blocking software**. This special software allows you to block access to sites that contain undesirable content.

- Set the 'Content Advisor rating' in Windows® XP. This is like the filtering/blocking software mentioned above but is already built-in to Windows®. To set it:

1 Click on 'Start'.
2 Right click in 'Internet Explorer'.
3 Select 'Internet Properties'.
4 Click on the 'Content' tab as shown.

5 Click on 'Enable'.
  The following screen is displayed (see picture on next page).
6 You can now select a rating for each of the four categories (language, nudity, sex and violence) ranging from 0, which filters out a lot of it, to 4, which allows you to see everything.

Hints and tips
As there is so much undesirable content on the Internet, these filters are not very effective. It is recommended that you buy specialist filtering/blocking software if you are particularly concerned about it.

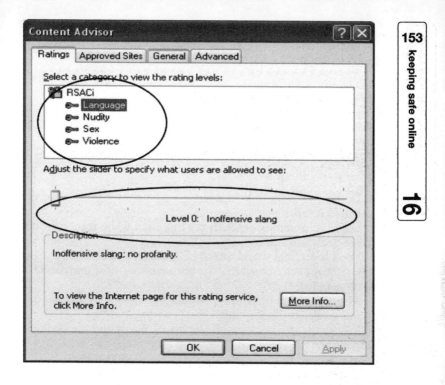

16.6 Premium diallers

A **premium dialler** is a piece of software that installs itself onto your computer. Next time you log on to the Internet it will not use your normal number to connect, but will dial a premium rate service charging up to £1.50 a minute. This is legal as the software does not install itself without you knowing it – you will see a message that asks you if you want to install it. However, the message is not clearly worded so you may click 'Yes' not really understanding what you are signing up to.

This is a tricky scam as you often see messages popping up when you are on the Internet, and most of them are fairly benign. You are most likely to encounter a premium dialler scam on download sites. These are sites where you can get free software.

What to do about it:

• Read all messages carefully before clicking 'Yes' whenever you are on the Internet.

- Phone BT and ask them to block all outgoing calls to premium rate numbers.
- Only use reputable sites.

16.7 Unreliable sites

Many of the problems described in this chapter come from unreliable sites. But how do you spot a dodgy site? It is not always easy as even bad websites can be made to look good.

What to do about it:

- Don't click on a **link** to a website that comes from an unsolicited email.
- Use your common sense. If it's too good to be true, then it's probably a scam.
- Look for a 'real world' presence, preferably an address.
- Use only sites of well-known businesses or sites that are recommended.
- Avoid sites that offer free downloads, free movies, free music, free games or **file-sharing**.
- Ensure the site is secure – look for the https and the padlock symbol.

16.8 Buying online

When you buy anything online there is always a danger that the goods will not be delivered, or that what is delivered, is not what you ordered.

What to do about it:

- Buy only from trusted websites. This could be the websites of large companies or those that have been recommended by a friend.
- Keep copies of all receipts. All decent online stores will provide a screen where you can print a copy of your order. Most will also send an email to confirm the order.
- Check for a real address so that you can contact them if something goes wrong. It is preferable if they are located in the same country as you!
- Use your common sense. If a deal looks too good to be true – it probably is.
- Have a separate credit/debit card that you use for online transactions and have only a small credit limit on it.

- Use secure payment services such as **PayPal**. These provide insurance against non-delivery.

16.9 Passwords

Passwords usually in combination with a **user name** are required all over the place. Your computer itself will probably require a user name and password. Email sites, online auctions, **chat rooms**, etc. all require you to register with a user name and password.

Passwords are very important and keep you safe online. There are some rules that you should follow:

- Never ever give your password to anyone else.
- Change your password regularly and don't use the same password twice.
- Don't choose something obvious like names, dates of birth, etc. Use combinations of letters, numbers and other characters, as they are harder to guess.
- Don't write passwords down anywhere.

16.10 Don't have nightmares . . .

Internet crime is increasing and you are never immune to threats even if you take all of the precautions listed in this chapter. However, if you take precautions, the chances of becoming a victim are small. Remember that millions of people now use the Internet regularly with no problems.

Summary
In this chapter we have discussed:
- What threats exist on the Internet
- How to protect yourself against them
- How to identify unreliable or undesirable websites
- Advice on buying online
- Advice on using passwords

17

getting photographs from your digital camera onto your computer

In this chapter you will learn:

- how to connect the camera to the computer
- how to copy images from the camera to the computer
- browsing and editing photographs
- printing photographs

17.1 Introduction

When you take a photograph with a digital camera, the photo is stored on a **card** that is stored inside the camera itself. Eventually this card will get full of photographs and your camera will not let you take any more pictures. When this happens, you need to delete some of the photos. However, if you do this, those photographs become permanently deleted (i.e. they are gone forever).

What you need to do, therefore, is copy the photographs from the camera and store them on your computer. This process is sometimes referred to as **uploading**. Your computer's 'hard disk' has a much larger storage capacity than your camera so you will be able to store thousands of photographs on your computer.

Also, once the photographs are on the computer you can do other things with them. The most common thing you might want to do is print them out. However, you can also edit them, perhaps adjusting the brightness or contrast of individual photographs.

17.2 Getting started

There are hundreds of different digital cameras available. When you buy a digital camera, you will be supplied with a CD that contains special **software** that is needed to upload the photographs from the camera. There are lots of different makes of software. This chapter uses one of the most common brands called Camedia, which is supplied with Olympus cameras.

The software also contains lots of other features such as a **browse** option, which lets you view all of the photographs stored on your computer or camera. The software will also allow you to edit the photographs.

17.3 Connecting the camera to the computer

First, you need to connect the camera to the computer. This is done using a lead that will have been provided when you bought the camera. One end of the lead plugs into the camera and the other end plugs into one of the **USB ports**.

1 Connect your camera to your computer.
2 Now switch on the camera.

Most cameras have two settings. You should switch it to the setting that allows you to view the photographs you have taken, rather than the one that allows you to take photographs.

On some cameras, you have to press a button on the camera to tell it that it is connected to the computer.

Hints and tips
Digital cameras use up batteries quickly so don't leave your camera on unnecessarily. You can buy power adapters so that you can plug them into the mains.

17.4 Opening the camera software

You now need to open the software that was supplied with the camera.

1 Open the software for the camera. In this case, it is the Camedia software.
2 The software will now **load** and you will be presented with the opening **menu**. In the case of Camedia it looks like this (see picture on next page top).
   If you are using different software, the screen will not look like this, but there should be an option to 'Browse' or 'Transfer' images.
3 Click on 'Transfer'.
   This option transfers the images from the camera to the computer. One of two things will happen now. If everything is working correctly, you will see a screen that displays all of the photographs on the camera. These are shown as **thumbnails,** which means that you can see lots of them on one screen.

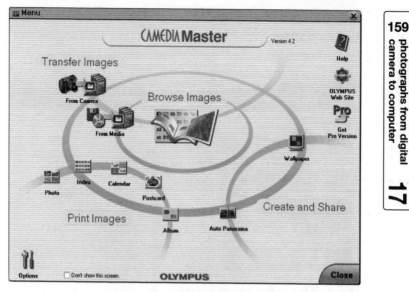

There is a possibility that the computer will not recognize that the camera has been plugged in. If this is the case, you will see a message saying that the camera can't be found.

If this happens:

4 Disconnect and then reconnect the camera, and make sure it is switched on. Check the LCD screen on the camera as it may be giving you instructions too.

17.5 Uploading (saving) the photographs

You now need to tell it where to upload (save) the images. For now, you can upload them to the My Pictures **folder**, which is already set up for you. Chapter 19 provides more information on how to organize your work into folders.

1 Find the folder called 'My Pictures' and click on it:

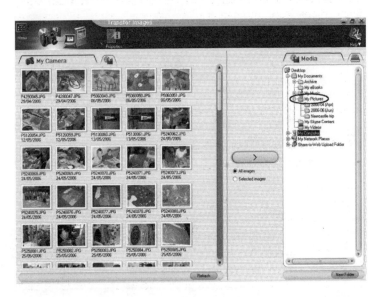

You can now select all of the images on the camera, or just selected ones.

If you want only selected images:

2 Click on each thumbnail image that you want to upload and then select the 'Selected images' option.

To upload all of the images:

3 Select the 'All images' option.

The photographs are now transferred from the camera into the My Pictures folder. A message will be displayed indicating when the transfer is complete.

4 Switch off the camera and disconnect it from the computer.

Hints and tips

You will notice that your photographs have strange names e.g. PIC0010. You can rename these later. Chapter 19 tells you how to do this.

17.6 Deleting photographs from your camera

Once the photos have been uploaded successfully, you can safely delete them from the camera. All cameras have an option to delete individual photographs or all photographs in one go. This varies from camera to camera.

Another thing you might want to do from time to time is to create a separate copy of all of your photographs just in case they accidentally get lost or deleted from you computer. There is more information on this in Chapter 20.

17.7 Browsing and editing photographs

There are lots of ways that you can view your photographs. In Chapter 19 you will be shown how you can use Windows® XP to browse through your photograph collection. You will also be able to browse through photographs using the camera software, in this case Camedia.

1   In your camera software, select 'Browse'.
2   This will show you a thumbnail and enlarged view of each photograph. In Camedia it looks like this:

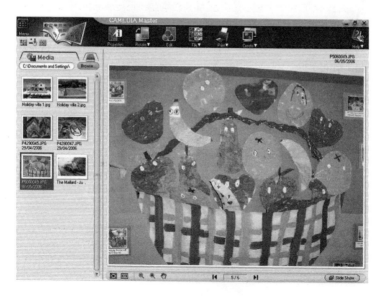

The thumbnails are shown down the left and when you click on a thumbnail, a larger version of the photograph is shown in the larger window.

You can edit (change) the photograph at this point if necessary. For example, the image may be too dark, or you may feel that there is not enough contrast between the colours. Most software also has a red-eye reduction option.

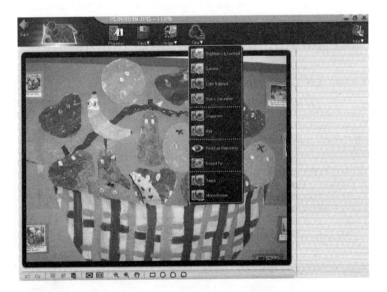

You might like to experiment with some of these options. It will change the image instantly so you can see what effect the change has. When complete, you need to save any changes you have made.

17.8 Printing photographs

You can print out your photographs either from the camera software or from Windows® XP. To print from the camera software:

> **Hints and tips**
> Some cameras come with a printer and all you have to do is plug your camera straight into the printer.

1 Select the photograph you want to print.
2 Select 'File' and 'Print' from the menu or click on the 'Print' icon from the toolbar.

To print from Windows® XP:

1 Click on 'Start' and select 'My Pictures'.
2 Right click on the photograph you want to print and select 'Print'.

Modern printing techniques mean that you will get a good quality image even if printing on standard A4 photocopier paper. Alternatively, you can pay more for photo quality paper.

163
photographs from digital
camera to computer

17

Hints and tips
Printed photographs often fade quite quickly on standard paper, so if you want the photograph to last, photo quality paper is recommended.

Summary
In this chapter we have discussed:
- How to connect your camera to your computer
- How to transfer photographs from a digital camera to the computer
- How to browse through images
- How to access the editing options
- How to print photographs

18

scanning traditional photographs into your computer

In this chapter you will learn:

- how to use a scanner
- how to scan photographs
- how to adjust photographs
- how to save photographs on the computer
- how to adjust the quality (resolution) of the image
- how to use 'one-touch' scanning

Aim of this chapter
This chapter will show you how to scan traditional colour or black and white photographs and save them onto your computer so that you have a digital version of them. This involves the use of a flatbed scanner, which is designed specifically to turn things on paper into a digital format that can be viewed and edited on the computer.

18.1 Introduction

A **flatbed scanner** turns a paper-based image into a digital one on the computer. There are many situations where you might want to scan an image. For example, if you find an image in a book and would like to use it on the computer, or as in this case, if you have old photographs that you would like to store on the computer. You can scan anything you like – it does not have to be an image. The process is exactly the same.

The advantage of scanning an image is that although your photographs may fade over time, or become damaged, a digital image is relatively secure on your computer.

In order to scan, you must have a scanner. This chapter assumes that you have one and that it is ready to use on the computer. If you have just bought a new scanner and have not plugged it in yet, see Chapter 5 for instructions on how to install it.

18.2 Getting started

When you buy a scanner, it will come with its own **software**. In this chapter, the Hewlett-Packard Photo and Imaging software will be used. This might not be the same as the scanner software that you have although the features will be exactly the same.

1 Check that your scanner is plugged in, switched on and connected to your computer.
2 Lift the lid of the scanner.
3 Place the photograph face down on the top right-hand corner of the glass plate.
4 Close the lid.

Hints and tips
Scanners use light reflection so it is important that the lid is closed, otherwise you will get lots of black on your images.

5 Now open your scanner software either from the **desktop** or the Start **menu**. Some scanners have a 'one-touch' scanning option. This means that there is a button on the scanner, which will do this bit for you. Check if your scanner has this. There are more details on this at the end of this chapter.

The Hewlett-Packard software looks like this. Yours may look different from this but will have similar options.

For example, it will open the My Pictures **folder** and show you all of the pictures that are in there. In this example, there are two photographs of a holiday villa.

Across the top there are options including the 'Scan' option that we will be using shortly.

Down the left-hand side is a **folders tree,** which shows all of the folders that have been set up on your computer. The My Pictures folder is one that already exists and it is stored inside the My Documents folder. Your computer will not have all the same folder names as this. There is more advice on using folders to store photographs in the next chapter.

18.3 Scanning an image

1 Click on 'Scan'.

A scan **preview** screen will now be displayed. Again, it may not look exactly the same as the one shown below, but it will show you a preview of the photograph that you have scanned. The purpose of the preview is to show you what the image will look like when it is saved. If there is anything wrong with it, you need to adjust it now.

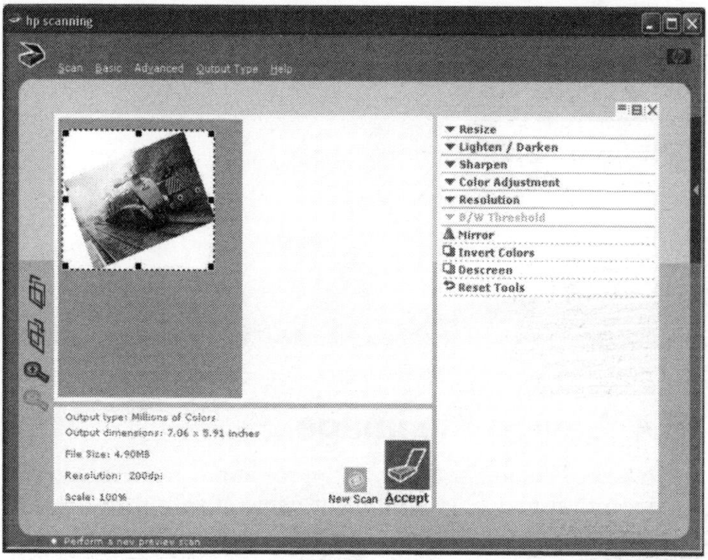

2 In the example above, the photograph is not on straight, so it needs scanning again. You would need to lift the lid and straighten the photograph on the glass, and then click 'Scan' again (see picture on next page).

There are many photograph editing options that you might want to experiment with. For example, it is possible to adjust the lightness/darkness or the colour contrast of the photograph at this point. As you adjust the settings, the preview will change to show you the effect of the adjustments.

In most cases, none of these adjustments will be necessary and you can save the image straight away.

Hints and tips
Your scanner will work to standard settings, which are perfectly adequate for most purposes.

18.4 Saving the image

1 To accept the image that you can see in the preview, click on 'Accept'. It may have a different name in your software, but the process is the same.

It will then scan the image again with the final settings, which you may or may not have changed.

You may be asked to select a **file name** and **file type** at this stage.

2 The file type should normally be set to '**jpg**', which is a standard format for photographs.

3 You can give the file any file name you like. As when saving any files, it is best to give it a meaningful name that you can recognize later on. In this case the file is called: The Mallard - June 1998

Hints and tips

You might find it helpful to date the file name of your photographs for future reference. Some scanning software creates new folders automatically with the current date on them.

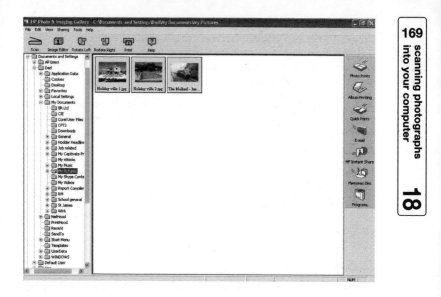

When the scan is complete, the photograph you have just scanned is displayed in the folder. This view is known as a thumbnail view.

You can now continue by putting the next photograph on the scanner and so on.

18.5 Problems with file size and resolution

Every time a file is saved on your computer, it takes up some space on the **hard disk** where all files are stored. Photographs are stored in files and take up a lot of space. If you also use a digital camera, you will have come across this problem already, in that you can store only a limited number of photographs on the camera at any one time.

This is not necessarily a problem if you have a computer with a big hard disk (e.g. anything over 40GB). However, if you plan to store thousands of photographs, you might run out of space. Another problem is that if you want to send photographs to other people (perhaps as email **attachments**), then large files take much longer to send.

To give you an idea, a typical good quality scanned photograph will take up 1000 times more space than a typical Word document.

In Chapter 2, the idea of **resolution** was introduced. On a digital camera, you can choose between high resolution and low resolution (and often a few other settings in-between). High resolution images are better quality but take up much more space on your camera and on your computer.

When you scan an image, you can set the resolution to whatever you like ranging from 75dpi (dots per inch) to several thousand; 90dpi is sufficient for most photographs even though your scanner software will probably be set to 200–300dpi.

Hints and tips

dpi is a measure of the quality of an image. It stands for dots per inch. Funny that something so high-tech should be measured in imperial units!

To change the resolution:

1 Click on 'Settings'. This may be called Scanner Setting or Scanner Properties on your software.
2 Find the 'Resolution' setting and select '90dpi' from the list.
3 Save the settings.

Next time you scan, it will scan at this new lower setting.

18.6 One-touch scanning

Many modern scanners now have a one-touch scanning facility. This means that there will be a button on the scanner, which when pressed will automatically open the scanner software and scan the image for you. This will work to the standard settings.

The disadvantage is that you have less control over the settings, but if you are happy with the standard settings (which are fine in most cases), then this option will save you some time.

Summary

In this chapter we have discussed:
• How to use a scanner including 'one-touch' scanning
• How to scan photographs
• How to adjust the settings including the resolution (quality) of the image
• How to preview and then save a scanned image

19 keeping track of your photographs and other files

In this chapter you will learn:

- where photographs are stored on the computer
- how to create folders in which to store photographs
- how to move photographs into new folders
- how to view several photographs at the same time using thumbnails
- how to rename photographs
- how to delete photographs

Aims of this chapter

This chapter will show you how to keep track of all of your photographs and other files by knowing where they are on your computer and what they are called. It is likely that over a period of a few years, you could end up with hundreds or thousands of photographs. This chapter will show you how to create new folders and rename photographs so that you can access them easily. It will also show you how to use the thumbnail view so that you can view several photographs at the same time.

Although this chapter uses photographs as an example, exactly the same principle applies to all other files such as all of your Word documents.

19.1 Introduction

You may already have lots of photographs on your computer, either from your digital camera, or from traditional photographs you have scanned, or even photographs that people have sent you via email.

Most photographs will end up in a **folder** called My Pictures which is a **subfolder** within the My Documents folder. This is because when you **download** photographs or scan them, the **software** that you use will often put them into this folder. This is all right, but after a while you could have hundreds of photographs in this folder, which makes it difficult to keep track of them all.

This chapter will show you how to use Windows® XP to manage all of your photographs. The skills learned in this chapter can be applied to the management of any type of **files** – not just photographs.

19.2 Getting started

To start with, make sure that you have got some photographs on your system that you can use.

In this example, there are several photographs in the My Pictures folder, which we are going to rename and then move into a new folder that will be created for them.

1 From the **Windows desktop**, click on the 'Start' **menu** and select 'My Documents'.

A window will open that will look like this. This is displaying the contents of the folder. In this case, there are a number of folders already within the folder, most of which you will have on your computer too. For example, the My Pictures and My Music folders will be on your computer and you may have some of the others too. Every computer will be different so don't worry if you do not have all of these folders.

Hints and tips
A folder on the computer is just like a real folder. It is somewhere to store information.

---

2 Double click on 'My Pictures' and another window will open showing the contents of the My Pictures folder (see picture on next page).
   You are now inside a folder, that itself is inside a folder. This can get confusing. If you get lost at any time:
3 Click on the 'Back' button in exactly the same way as when using the **Internet**. This will take you back to the folder before.

It might help to think of it like a family tree. At the top of the tree is My Documents and then everything else branches off from that.

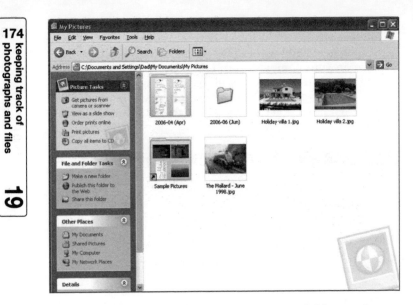

In this example above, there are some more folders and some actual photographs.

19.3 Using the thumbnail view

The **thumbnail** view is really useful and is used in all sorts of circumstances on a computer. It means that several small images are displayed on the same screen allowing you to see a small (thumbnail) version of the image.

In the example above, there are only a few images in the folder so you can see them all on the one screen. If there were more, you might have to **scroll down** in the window in order to see them all.

To see a larger version of an image, double click on it (see picture on next page).

When you have viewed the image, click on the cross in the top right-hand corner of this window and you are taken back to the My Pictures folder.

19.4 Renaming a file

All information is stored in a file. Whether you are saving a letter, poster or photograph, they are all stored in files. It is often useful to rename the files so that the **file name** makes more sense.

Most digital cameras automatically give each photograph a file name, and this file name is usually something pretty useless like PIC0000111. To rename a file, you can view the thumbnail of it and then rename it with a name that is appropriate to the image.

In the example below, a new file has been added from the digital camera. The camera has called it P1010203.

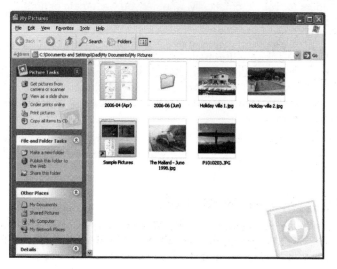

To rename the file:

1 Right click on the image.
2 Select 'Rename' from the list.
3 You can now type in a sensible name, for example: Angel of
   the North.jpg

It is important that you type the **.jpg** bit as this is what tells the computer that it is a photograph.

If you had lots of files, perhaps if you have just downloaded lots from your digital camera, you could have a session on the computer where you just work your way through renaming all the files.

19.5 Creating new folders

Another useful way of keeping track of photographs (or any other kind of file for that matter) is to create folders within the My Pictures folders for different sets of photos.

For example, you might have a folder called Holiday Pictures, one called Family Pictures, etc., or you might create a folder using the date as a name as has been done in the case above.

Hints and tips
Some software for digital cameras and **scanners** will create these folders for you automatically, whether you want them or not!

The problem with using dates for folder names is that it is unlikely that you will remember when the photos were taken, so after a while the folder name becomes pretty useless. If your software does create folders for you using dates, then rename them in exactly the same way as you rename a file, using the right click and Rename option.

To create a new folder:

1 Right click anywhere where there is white space in the folder.
2 This will display a menu.

Hints and tips
The right click options vary depending on where you right click. To create a new folder, you must right click somewhere in the folder, but not on a file.

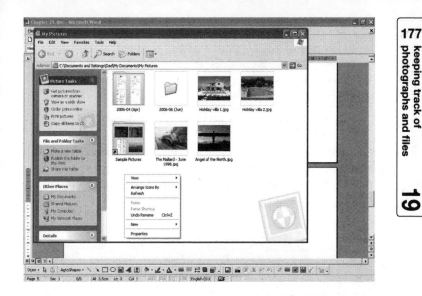

3 Select 'New' and then select 'Folder'.

4 A new folder is created within the current folder called 'New Folder'.

5 Type in a new name for this folder, for example: Newcastle trip 2006.

You now have a folder that you can use to put in all of the photographs from this particular trip. The folder name is useful as it will help you to remember what is in the folder at a later date.

19.6 Moving files into folders

It would make sense to create any new folders before you start downloading images. Then you can tell the computer to put the images straight into your new folder.

It is also possible to move files around between folders and to have several copies of the same file in different folders.

Hints and tips

It is best just to have one copy of every file on your computer as it makes it easier to know where they are.

To move a file:

1 Right click on the file that you want to move. In this example, we will move the Angel of the North.jpg file into the Newcastle trip folder.
2 Select 'Cut' from the list.
3 Double click on the Newcastle trip folder.
This will now open this folder, which at the moment will not have anything it.
4 Right click in the white space at the bottom of the window.
5 Right click, and select 'Paste'.

The photograph is then moved from the My Pictures folder into the Newcastle trip folder.

This folder may be set up with a different view. It may look like this:

This is called the **Filmstrip view** and is quite useful as it shows the thumbnail across the bottom, with a larger image at the top.

To switch between these different views:

Select 'View' from the menus and click on 'Thumbnail' or 'Filmstrip' depending on which you prefer.

You might want to experiment with the other views while you are here.

19.7 Deleting a file

If you ever want to delete a file completely, you can do this from here. Deleting a file permanently removes it from your computer. You might choose to delete files if you don't want to keep them (e.g. a particularly embarrassing photo), or if you already have the file somewhere else, or if you start to run out of space on your computer.

To delete a file:

1 Right click on the file you want to delete.
2 Click 'Delete'.
3 Click 'OK' when it asks if you are sure.

Hints and tips
Remember that deleting a file gets rid of it completely. You won't be able to get it back again.

19.8 Understanding the folder structure

Getting to grips with the folder structure is complicated. There are already hundreds of folders on your computer used to store all of the files for the software that you are running. Every time you install new software, a new batch of folders will be created. Folders within folders within folders . . .

You do have to be careful when exploring your folders that you don't move anything or delete it unless you are absolutely sure what it is. This could stop your computer from working properly.

The best approach is to only use the My Documents folder as a start point and to put all of your files into this folder OR sub-folders within it. You can create as many sub-folders as you like. You will have to remember what you have put into all these sub-folders so give them sensible names.

A different view of the folders is shown here.

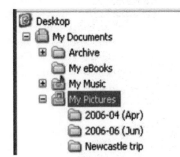

It shows the family tree idea mentioned before. At the top is the Desktop, then the My Documents folder branches off from this. One of the folders within it is the My Pictures folder and within that there are three further folders including the Newcastle trip folder used in the example.

You can see how quickly the folder structure grows when you are using your computer. For new users of computers, this is often one of the hardest things to understand, so don't worry if you haven't quite got it yet. Every time you save a file of any sort, you will see the folder structure again, which is another chance to get to grips with it!

Summary

In this chapter we have discussed:

- How to create and rename folders
- How to rename files
- How to move files
- How to change the folder view
- How to understand the folder structure

20

copying files onto CD, DVD and memory stick

In this chapter you will learn:

- what a backup is and why you need to do it
- how to make a copy of your work
- how to copy information onto DVD, CD and memory stick

Aim of this chapter
The aim of this chapter is to show you how you can create copies of any kind of file on your computer. It will explain why you might want to create a copy in the first place, and go on to explain the process of copying onto different types of storage devices including CD, DVD and memory stick.

20.1 Introduction

There are several reasons why you might want to create a copy of your work. The main reason is to create a **backup** so that if anything goes wrong on your computer, you still have the **files** stored elsewhere.

You might also want to **copy** files onto a portable device such as a CD, DVD or **memory stick** so that you can move files from one computer to another, or if you want to give someone else a copy of something that you have done on your computer.

If you **download** music, video or **software** from the **Internet,** you could create a copy on a CD or DVD so that you can keep a safe copy of it.

20.2 Creating a backup

A backup is a complete separate version of a file or files that are stored onto a separate device away from the computer. The purpose of a backup is so that if you lose any of the files on your computer for whatever reason, you still have a safe copy somewhere that you can then put back onto your computer.

Files can get deleted by accident, or destroyed by a **virus,** or your computer could crash and destroy files. The first one on this list is actually the most likely. You can create a backup as often as you like. You should probably aim to do one at least once a month. You do not need to backup everything on your computer, just your own work.

In Chapter 19, you looked at how you can create **folders** within the My Documents folder in which to store your work. Doing it this way makes it easier to know which files and folders to backup as you can simply backup everything that is contained within My Documents.

There are different ways of creating a backup, but the most common is to backup onto CD or DVD. In Chapter 2 we looked at buying either a DVD or CD writer for this purpose – this is the tray that opens up into which you place the CD or DVD.

> **Hints and tips**
> Although DVD is associated with films, they can actually be used for storing any type of information.

This chapter assumes that you have either one of these. Most computers will have one or the other, not usually both. The process for creating a backup is the same regardless. You will also need to have some CDs or DVDs onto which to create the backup. These must be CD-R, CD-RW, DVD-R or DVD-RW.

- **CD-R** and **DVD-R** disks can have files copied onto them once. You can put only one set of files on them but you can copy the files back from the CD at any time.
- **CD-RW** and **DVD-RW** disks can be used over and over again. This means that you can use the same CD or DVD each time you backup.

> **Hints and tips**
> CD-R and DVD-R disks are cheaper to buy than the RW versions and are ideal for backups.

20.3 Selecting the files or folders to backup

In this example, parts of the My Documents folder will be backed up:

1 Open the CD/DVD tray by pressing the button located on the tower or desktop next to the tray itself.
2 Insert a blank CD or DVD into the drive, label up.
3 Press the button to close the CD/DVD tray.
4 Click on 'Start' and select 'My Documents'.
5 You can now select which folders and files you want to backup.

To select all the folders and files within My Documents:

6 You can either click and hold, and **drag** the **mouse pointer** across all of the folders, or you can press CTRL and A at the same time. The folders and files will be shown as selected as they go a dark blue colour.

To select specific files and folders:

7 Click on the file or folder that you want. If you want more than one, use CTRL and click at the same time. This allows you to select several files or folders one at a time. In this case, the whole of the My Documents folder will be backed up.

8 Press CTRL and A so that all files and folders are selected.

9 Right click on any of the selected folders or files and select 'Copy'.

10 Now click on the small arrow near the top of the window as shown:

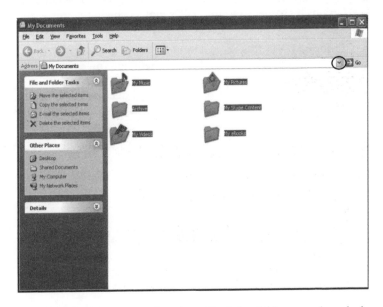

The folder structure showing all of the folders on the whole computer will now be displayed.

You want to copy these files onto the CD or DVD. This will be shown in the list. It will be called the CD or DVD Drive (depending on which one is on your computer), and will have a letter after it in brackets, for example (D:).

11 Select the CD or DVD Drive.

12 This will then take you to a new window, which displays the contents of the CD or DVD. As you have just put a new one in, there will be nothing on it and the window will be empty as shown:

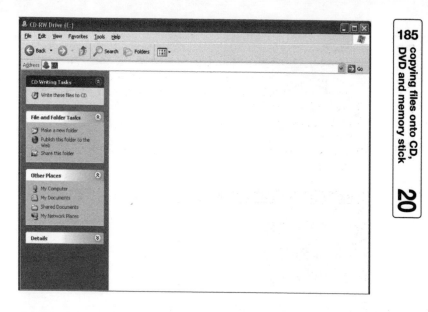

20.4 Pasting onto the CD or DVD

The next stage is to **paste** the files:

1 Right click anywhere in the white space of this window and select 'Paste'.
   This will paste all of the files/folders that you selected previously. You might get some messages about 'stream loss'. If you do, just click on 'Yes'.

2 On the left-hand side of this window, you will see a label that reads: 'Write these files to CD'. Click on this.

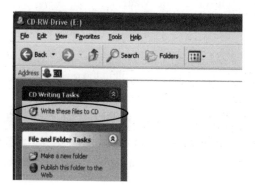

This will open the CD writing **wizard**, which looks like this:

CD Writing Wizard

Welcome to the CD Writing Wizard

This wizard helps you write, or record, your files to a CD recording drive.

Type the name you want to give to this CD, or just click Next to use the name below.

CD name:

Jun 14 2006

New files being written to the CD will replace any files already on the CD if they have the same name.

☐ Close the wizard after the files have been written

< Back   Next >   Cancel

3 You can put a title on your CD if you want to, or it will use the date if you don't. The title is useful later as it will be displayed when you view the CD. Click 'Next'.
   The backup will now begin. Depending on how many files and folders you have, this could take anywhere between a minute and ten minutes. When it has finished, it will automatically open the CD/DVD tray.
4 Remove the CD/DVD.
5 Write on the front of the disk so that you know what it is and put it somewhere safe, preferably away from the computer.
6 Click on 'Finish' on the wizard.

Hints and tips
You can buy special pens for writing onto the CD surface. Don't use stickers as these may come off in the drive.

20.5 Running out of space on the CD/DVD

CDs and DVDs have room for only a certain number of files and folders. To give you an idea, a medium **resolution** (quality) photograph taken on a digital camera takes up about 1 **megabyte** (1MB). A music track takes up about 5MB. Most CDs have about 750MB on them, which means that you could store 750 photographs or 150 music tracks on one CD. DVDs can store roughly 20 times as many.

If you do run out of room on a CD or DVD, you will get an error message telling you that the disk is full. If this is the case, you will have to go back and select fewer files and folders, and try again.

20.6 Copying music and video files

If you are creating a copy of a music or video file to give to someone else, or perhaps to use on a different computer, the process is exactly the same as described for making a backup.

20.7 Copying files to a memory stick

The picture shows a memory stick.

They are also known as memory keys, or USB storage devices. They plug into a **USB port** and can be used for storing files and folders. They are not usually used for backup purposes, but only when files need transferring between computers.

They are useful devices to have if you ever need to move files between computers. For example: you might do an evening class and want to use files on your home computer and then take them into class; you might have more than one computer in your house and want to move files between computers.

Memory stick versus floppy disk. You may be wondering why the **floppy disk** has not had a mention yet. Floppy disks are 3.5 inch disks that you slide into the slot in the front of your computer. You can save files onto them. The problem with the floppy disk is that you cannot save very big files onto them. Typically, they would store only one decent quality digital photograph. This is why most people now opt to buy a memory stick. You can buy different sizes of memory stick. They are physically all the same size, but some can store more files than others.

The process of saving folders and files onto the memory stick is similar to the process of backing up, and this section assumes you have already worked through that part of this chapter:

1 Plug the memory stick into one of the USB ports.
2 Open the 'My Documents' folder.
3 Select the files or folders that you want to copy.
4 Right click on any of the selected files/folders and select 'Copy'.
5 Click on the small drop down arrow near the top of the window to display the folder structure.
   The memory stick will be listed as Removable Disk, again with a letter in brackets.
6 Select 'Removable disk' and a new window is opened which shows the contents of your memory stick. If you have not used it before, it will be empty.
7 Now right click in the white space in this window and select 'Paste'.

The files/folders are now written onto the memory stick and you can close down all of the open windows.

20.8 Safe removal of the memory stick

You can now just unplug the memory stick, but it is safer to tell Windows® XP that you are doing it. You should always follow this routine when unplugging any device attached to a USB port.

In the bottom right-hand corner of the screen, on the **taskbar** there are a number of small **icons**.

1 Click on the small arrow as shown.

This will reveal further icons.

2 Click on the one with the small green arrow. When you hover the mouse Pointer over it, it will show the label 'Safely Remove Hardware'.

3 A small menu will be displayed listing all of the devices plugged into USB ports. Click on the one that reads 'Mass Storage Device'. Notice that the letter in brackets is there again so you know it is the right one.

4 You can now safely remove the memory stick from the USB port.

Summary

In this chapter we have discussed:

- What a backup is and why you should do it
- How to create a backup of folders and files onto CD or DVD
- How to copy and paste files onto a memory stick
- How to safely remove a memory stick

21

making cards for all occasions

In this chapter you will learn:

- how to use Microsoft® Publisher
- about different types of publication
- how to use the wizard to create an invitation card
- how to make changes to the invitation card
- how to save and print the invitation card

Aims of this chapter
This chapter is the first of three that cover the use of Microsoft®
Publisher. This will show you how you can use the wizard to automatically create one of the many different types of publication
available in the software – in this case an invitation to a party. After
you have used the wizard to create your invitation, you will be
shown how you can make changes to it. Finally, you will be shown
how to save and print the invitation.

21.1 Introduction

Microsoft® Publisher is what is called desktop publishing software (DTP). It works in a similar way to Microsoft® Word in that
you can mix text and images together to make a publication. The
big difference with Publisher is that it contains templates for hundreds of different types of publication including invitations,
posters, leaflets and even **websites**.

There are three different ways of using Publisher:

- Publications by **wizard** – this leads you through a set of screens
  asking you what publication you want and how you want it
  to look (this chapter looks at this method).
- Publications by design – this gives you a template (layout) to
  work with and you put the text and images that you want to
  use into the template.
- Blank publications – this is where you start with a blank screen
  (like you do in Word) and you have to create the layout and
  put all the text and images in from scratch.

You can choose which of these methods you want to use each
time you create a new publication. Over the next three chapters,
you will be shown all three methods.

Hints and tips
Using a wizard is the easiest method but gives you less flexibility
over how the finished publication will look.

21.2 Getting started

1 Open Publisher either from the **desktop**, or from the Start
  menu. The first screen will offer you the three methods of creating a publication as described previously:

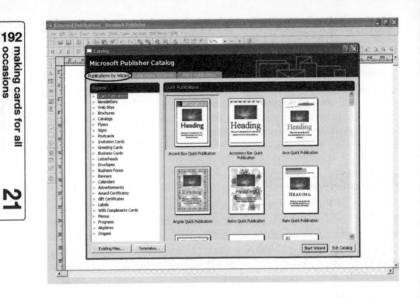

The Publication by Wizard option is the option that is currently available. You are presented with a long list of publication types. There are all different types of cards. In this case you will be creating an invitation although the principles explained here are the same for any type of card.

2 Select 'Invitation Cards' from the list.

A further list is then displayed of all of the different invitation cards that are available.

3 Select 'Celebration'.

In the main window you will see lots of **thumbnail** views of different layouts that are available. You can **scroll** through these to find one that you think is appropriate. For this example:

4 Select 'Anniversary Bells Invitation'.

5 Click the 'Start Wizard' button in the bottom right-hand corner of this screen.

The wizard will now lead you through several screens asking you for information that needs to be in the invitation. The first thing you will see is a screen that prompts you for your personal information:

6 Click 'OK' on this screen.

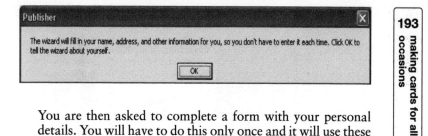

You are then asked to complete a form with your personal details. You will have to do this only once and it will use these details from then on in any publication that you make, if needed.

7 Complete the form. If there are any bits that are not relevant (e.g. logo), then leave these boxes blank.

A completed form would look something like this:

8 Click the 'Update' button when complete.

You now need to complete the rest of the invitation. The publication is shown in the main window and down the left-hand side of the screen is the wizard (see picture on next page top).

9 Click on 'Next' in the bottom left-hand corner.

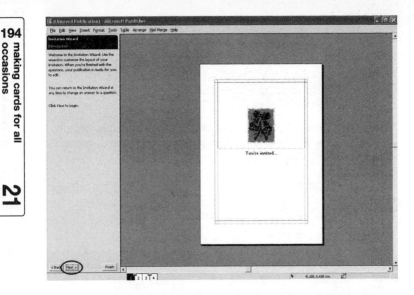

You are now presented with some options about how you want the layout to look. Some of these have weird and wonderful names that do not really mean much:

10 Click on the first of the options 'Juxtapositions'. In the main window, this will show you how this layout will look. You can now click through each of the options until you find the layout that you like the best.

Hints and tips
Some of these layouts use a lot of colour. You should bear this in mind if printing lots of copies, as it can be expensive in terms of printer ink.

11 In this example, select 'Art Bit' and click the 'Next' button. You are then prompted to select what type of fold you want. Again, some of these have odd names that do not really help you to understand what they mean.

12 Select the last option 'Half page side fold' and click 'Next'. This will print the invitation onto A4 paper in a format that allows you to put a single fold in it.

You are then prompted to select a colour scheme for the invitation. Colour schemes can be used to apply consistent colours to different parts of a publication. As you are making only one invitation, we can bypass this option for now.

13 Click 'Next'. The next option is for a 'Suggested Verse'. Because we are using the invitation wizard, it knows that you might want to add in a particular phrase, so it has come up with some for you:

14 Click 'Browse'.

The suggested phrases will now be shown:

Suggested Verse ☒

Category: [Anniversary Party ▼]

Available messages:
```
You're invited...
We're celebrating a heavenly ı
They've had fun for 25 years.
To honor 10 years of together
Come toast the happy couple.
Your presence is requested...
```

Front message:
```
Your presence is requested...
```

Inside message:
```
At an anniversary party.
```

[OK]   [Cancel]

If you click on each of the available messages, it will show you the message it will put on the front and on the inside of your publication.

15 For this example, click the last option and click 'OK'.

16 Now click 'Next'.

You are now prompted to select what personal information you wish to use. This is the personal information that you filled in earlier:

17 Select 'Home/Family' and click 'Finish'.

You have now finished using the wizard and your publication is complete. The wizard shows a screen that gives you the option of reviewing any of the stages and making any changes you think are necessary.

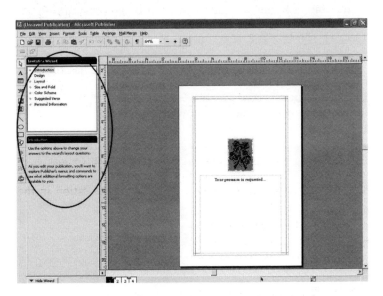

21.3 Making changes

For example, if you wanted to change the message:

1 Select 'Suggested Verse' from the list.
2 Select 'Browse' to see the options again.
3 Select a different verse and click 'OK'.

Your invitation is nearly complete, but there are a few more bits of information you need to type in. You have to do this yourself rather than using the wizard.

Click 'Hide Wizard' in the bottom left-hand corner. The left-hand window will disappear giving more room for your publication on the screen.

In the bottom left-hand corner you can see how many pages there are in the publication and what page you are on. This shows you that there are four pages. You have made an invitation in the form of a card, so:

- Page 1 is the front of the card.
- Pages 2 and 3 are the inside of the card.
- Page 4 is the back of the card.

21.4 Completing the card

You can now make changes to the invitation. You need to add some details to the inside of the invitation:

1   Click on '2' where shown above.
    This will show you the inside of the invitation (which are actually pages 2 and 3) (see picture on next page top).

You need to add more details about the party. You will notice how small the text is. In fact it is very hard to read.

2   Press the 'F9' key on your keyboard. This will zoom in to the invitation making it easier to read. Pressing 'F9' again will zoom back out.

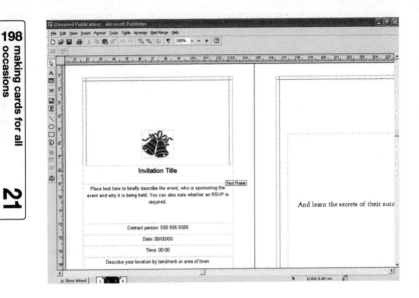

Hints and tips

F9 is really handy as you can zoom in when you need to see what you are typing and zoom out again to see how the overall layout is looking.

---

3 You now need to change the text putting in the details for your party.
   To change the text, you need to click on the piece of text that needs changing. This will highlight it in black and you can type your own text. For example:

4 Click on where it reads 'Invitation Title' and change this to 'Wedding Anniversary'.

5 Now go through and change the other text to customize the details to your party. An example is shown at the top of the next page.

Hints and tips

Typing in new text is just the same as when you type text into Microsoft® Word. Just click where you want to type – and type!

You could go on to make further changes if you wanted to, adding more text or more images, but for this example, the invitation is now finished.

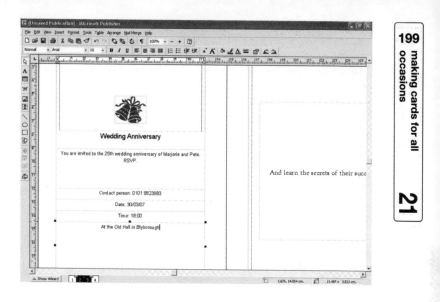

21.5 Saving your work

By now, you might have been prompted to save your work. Publisher has a habit of reminding you every ten minutes or so that you have not saved your work yet. You should save about every ten minutes to be on the safe side.

If you are prompted to save your work, then do so when prompted. Or:

1 Click on 'File' and 'Save' or on the 'Save' **icon.**
2 The file will be saved into the My Documents folder unless you tell it otherwise. Type in a suitable **file name,** for example 'Wedding Invitation' and click 'Save' (see picture at the top of the next page).

21.6 Printing your work

Printing from Publisher is pretty much the same as printing from any other **software** although you may have to put the publication together at the end. For example, when you type a letter, it prints onto A4 paper and you just fold it and send it. When printing an invitation like this, it will actually print out two sheets of A4 and you will have to put them together and fold them to create the card.

It is recommended that you print out the invitation first as this bit is easier to understand with one in front of you.

You have two options:

- Print out the invitation onto two sheets and then stick the two sheets back to back and fold in half to create the card.
- Print out the first sheet and then re-feed the paper into the printer so that it prints the second sheet on the other side of the same sheet of A4.

To print the invitation on two sheets of paper:

1 Click 'File' and 'Print' and select 'OK'.
  In this example, two sheets of A4 will be printed. The first is the front and back of the card and the second is the inside of the card.
2 Now stick the two sheets back to back.

To print the invitation on one sheet of paper:

1 Click 'File' and 'Print'.

The print options are now shown:

2 Rather than print both pages at the same time, click on 'Page' as shown and put 1 and 1 in both boxes. This just prints page 1.
3 When that has printed, take the printout and re-feed it into your printer so that you can print page 2 on the blank side.
4 Click 'Print' again and this time put 2 to 2 in the 'Pages' box. This will print page 2 only.

Hints and tips
All printers are different so there is no rule of thumb about which way to put in the paper to get it to print the right way round on the other side of the paper. It's a case of trial and error until you get it right.

---

5 When you have finished, click on the cross to close Publisher.

Summary
In this chapter we have discussed:
• How to use Microsoft® Publisher wizard
• How to create an invitation
• How to edit text
• How to print and save a publication

22

making a newsletter, leaflet or pamphlet

In this chapter you will learn:

- how to select a suitable template
- working in columns on the page
- how to use text and image frames
- how to get text to flow from one frame to the next

Aims of this chapter

This chapter is the second of three that cover the use of Microsoft® Publisher. In Chapter 21, you were introduced to the three ways in which Publisher can be used. This chapter focuses on creating 'Publication by Design', which means that you select a template and then fill it in with the text and images that you want.

This chapter will show you how you can use standard templates to create common publications such as newsletters, leaflets and pamphlets. It will also show you how to work with the chosen layout, adding text and images and getting the text to flow from one column to the next.

You should work through Chapter 21 before attempting this chapter.

22.1 Introduction

Some publications do not require much text, for example, invitations and cards. Other publications such as newsletters and pamphlets require a lot of text. They also tend to be laid out in columns so that the text flows from one column to the next – a bit like a newspaper.

This chapter will focus specifically on publications that use this type of format. The example used will be for a fund-raising newsletter although the skills learned here can be applied to other kinds of publication such as leaflets and pamphlets.

You can actually create a newsletter using the **wizard** that you learned in the previous chapter. For this example, though the wizard will not be used.

22.2 Getting started

1 Open Publisher either from the **desktop,** or from the Start **menu.**
   The first screen will offer you the three methods of creating a publication as described previously (see picture on next page).
2 Select the 'Publication by Design' option as shown.
   You are now presented with a long list of layout types.

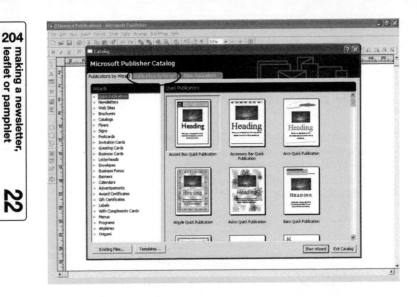

3 Select 'Fund-raiser Sets'.

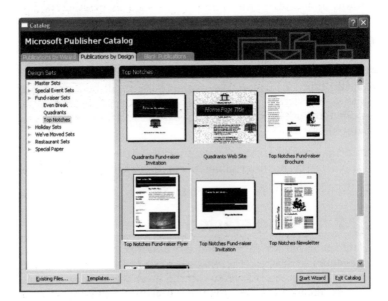

4 **Scroll** through the layout on the right until you find the one called 'Top Notches Newsletter'.

205
making a newsletter,
leaflet or pamphlet

22

5 Click on this and then select 'Start Wizard'.
   You can use the wizard here if you like, but the purpose of
   this chapter is to show you how to work without the wizard,
   so:
6 In the bottom left-hand corner, click 'Finish'. This will close
   the wizard.
7 Then click on 'Hide Wizard' to get rid of it completely.

Publisher has now presented us with a four-page newsletter and
it is displaying page 1. You can tell this because of the small page
references in the bottom left of the screen called 'Page navigation':

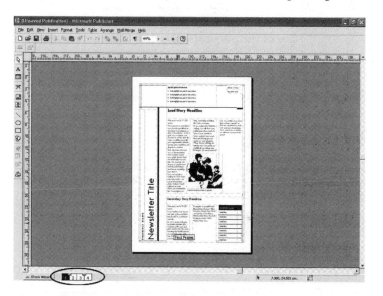

The advantage of using these layouts is that Publisher does a lot
of the work for you. However, there is still a lot left to do, as all
of the text and images need customizing.

22.3 Changing the text

Publisher uses **frames**. A frame can contain text or images. It uses
frames because it is easier to move the frames around to create
the desired layout. When you use Word, the text just appears on
the page. In Publisher, text needs to be put in a frame. When you
use one of Publisher's designs, some text is put into the frames
already, so that you can see what it will look like.

To change the text:

Click in the frame that contains the text. In this case, click in the frame at the top of the publication.

All of the text in that frame is then **highlighted**. You can now type in the text that you want to appear in this part of the publication.

The principle is the same now for any of the text frames.

22.4 Formatting text

When you were using Word, you got used to the idea of changing the style and size of the **font**. You can do this within Publisher too in a similar way.

1 Click on the frame that contains the text you want to change.
2 From the **toolbar** at the top, select the font style and size that you want.
3 You can also change the font colour on this toolbar.

22.5 Changing an image

Images are also put into frames. When you use one of Publisher's designs it will put in some images for you. These are from the **ClipArt** library. You can put your own image in either by:

- selecting a different ClipArt image
- copying and pasting an image from somewhere else
- inserting an image from a **file**.

To change a ClipArt Image:

1 Double click on the frame that contains the image. The ClipArt library will now **load**.
2 Search and select another image and insert it as described in Chapter 7.
3 Close the ClipArt library. The new image is now inserted.

To **copy and paste** an image:

1 Locate the image that you want to use. For example, you may have found a suitable image on a **web page**. Right click on it and select 'Copy'.
2 Right click in the publication on the image that you want to replace, and click 'Paste'.
  The image in the frame will be replaced with the new image.

To insert an image stored in a file:

1 Click once on the image in the publication that you want to replace.
2 Select 'Insert' from the menu and select 'Picture' and 'From File'. You can now select an image from your My Pictures folder. This will then replace the image in the frame.

22.6 Moving and re-sizing images

Publisher uses what is called **text wrapping**. This means that it will automatically move text to fit around an image. If you move an image or re-size it, the text will automatically adjust itself.

To re-size an image:

1 Click on it.
2 Move the **mouse pointer** to one of the four corners of the image until the mouse pointer changes to a diagonal arrow.
3 Left click and hold and then **drag** the corner so that the image re-sizes.
4 When you have achieved the size you want, let go of the left mouse button.

To move an image:

1 Click on the image and hold. The mouse pointer will say 'Move'.
2 While holding the left mouse button down, move the picture to its new location and then release the left mouse button.

An alternative to this is to use the arrow keys to move an image. This can be useful as it is a little more precise than using the mouse.

1　Click on the image.
2　Now use the ARROW KEYS in the direction that you want the image to move.

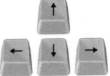

You will notice that the image moves by very small amounts allowing you to position it exactly where you want it.

22.7 Flowing text

This layout uses three columns like a standard newspaper. The way we read these is to read to the end of column 1, then start at the top of column 2 and so on.

The text in the three columns is linked together so that if you add more text, it will adjust itself to fit across the columns.

For example:

1　Click on the column to the left of the image as shown:

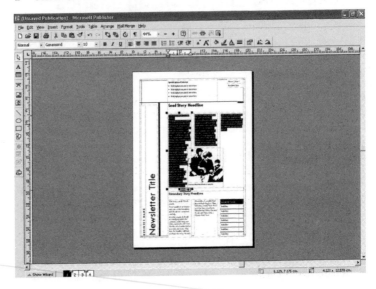

Notice how all three columns become highlighted. This is because these three text frames are linked together.

2 Press F9 to zoom in.
3 Press the LEFT ARROW KEY on the keyboard.

This moves the **cursor** to the start of this text so that you can edit it.

4 Type in 'This is an experiment to show how the text flows between the three columns'.

As you do this, you will notice that the text is continually adjusting itself so that it can fit in everything you are typing.

22.8 Deleting frames

It may be that you want to delete complete frames. If you are using one of Publisher's designs, as in this case, you might find that there are whole frames that you just don't want.

To delete them:

1 Click on the frame.
2 Right click and select 'Delete Object'. This will delete the frame and everything in it.

22.9 Adding frames

It may be that you need to add new frames. Perhaps you want to add a new image, or you have run out of space in one of the text boxes.

To add a text frame:

1 Click on the 'A' **icon** on the left-hand side of the screen as shown (see picture on next page).
2 Now move the mouse pointer onto the publication wherever you want this new text frame to go. You now need to click and hold the left mouse button while dragging out the frame.
3 When you have got the frame the size you want it, release the left mouse button.

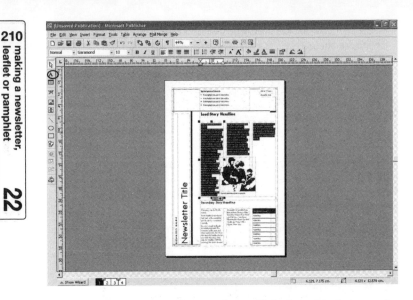

4   You can now move the text frame if the location is not quite right.

Adding a new image frame is the same process except you click on the 'Image' icon rather than the A as shown.

22.10 Deleting pages

You may also wish to delete whole pages. For example, this template provided you with a four-page newsletter. It may be that you only want a single page. If this is the case, you need to delete pages 2, 3 and 4 completely.

To do this:

1   Go to page 2 by clicking on the 'Page navigation' icon in the bottom left-hand corner.
2   Now select 'Edit' from the menu option across the top.
3   Select 'Delete Page'.
    As there are two pages here it will ask you whether you want to delete one or both of the pages.
4   Select 'Both pages' and click 'OK' (as shown on the next page).

5 You can follow the same process for any further pages you wish to delete.

Hints and tips
If you find that you are making lots of changes to one of the standard layouts, you might be better off starting your publication from scratch as described in the next chapter.

Summary
In this chapter we have discussed:
- How to use one of Publisher's newsletter templates
- How to work with text and image frames
- How text flows from one frame to another
- How to work with columns
- How to add and delete frames
- How to delete pages

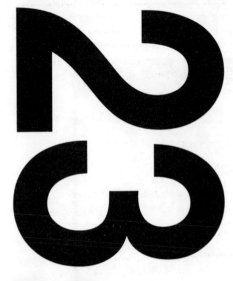

23 making a poster

In this chapter you will learn:

- how to design and create a new publication from scratch
- how to add text frames
- how to add WordArt frames
- how to add ClipArt and picture frames

Aim of this chapter

This chapter is the third of three that cover the use of Microsoft® Publisher. In Chapter 21, you were introduced to the three ways in which Publisher can be used. This chapter focuses on starting with a blank publication and adding the frames to include the text and images that you want.

You should work through Chapters 21 and 22 before attempting this chapter.

23.1 Introduction

This chapter will start from scratch with a blank page onto which you add what you want. It is possible to create a poster using the other two methods discussed in Chapters 21 and 22, but for the purposes of this chapter, a blank publication will be used.

As you know Publisher uses **frames,** so the basic rule is that you add the frame (box) first, and then you put the text or image into the frame.

23.2 Getting started

1   Open Publisher either from the **desktop,** or from the Start **menu.** The first screen will offer you the three methods of creating a publication as described previously:

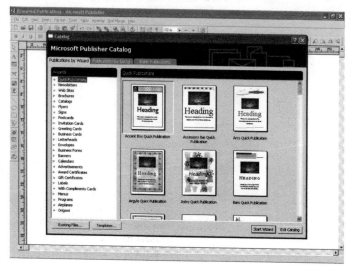

2 Select the 'Blank Publication' option as shown.
   You are now prompted to select the page format that you want.
3 Select 'Full Page' and click 'Create'.

Hints and tips
This example is for an A4-sized poster. It is possible to create larger posters using the 'Poster' option. This will print over several pages of A4 and then you have to assemble it yourself.

---

4 Click the 'Hide Wizard' button as you will not be using the **wizard** at all in this chapter.

This poster will be for an up-and-coming play, which will take place in the village hall. It will include a title, some images

and some text explaining what the play is all about. The finished poster is shown here, so this is what you are working
towards.

23.3 Adding a title using WordArt

To start with, add the title. This is using **WordArt**, which is available in all Microsoft® **software** and allows you to create visual
effects with words.

1   Click on the 'WordArt' **icon** on the right-hand side of the
    screen as shown below.

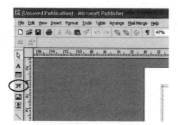

2   Now move the **mouse pointer** across the top of the page and
    left click and hold while you **drag** out a frame big enough to
    fit in the title. Don't worry if you don't get the size quite right
    as you can always re-size it later on.

Hints and tips
Use the light blue and pink borders as a guide. These allow room
for a white margin around the printed page.

---

3   When you release the mouse button, the WordArt options
    will be displayed (see picture on next page).
4   Where it reads 'Your Text Here', type in the title. In this case:
    An Inspector Calls.

The menus at the top of the screen have now changed. These are
the WordArt menus. To create the bendy effect:

5   Click on the little arrow to the right of where it reads 'Plain
    text'.

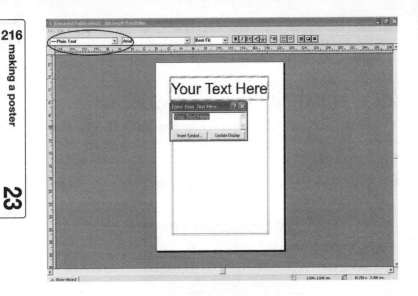

6 You can now select from a range of WordArt styles. The one
   used in this example is called Wave 1 and is the one circled.
   Click on this.

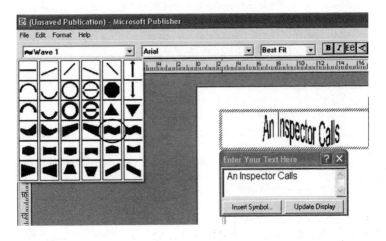

Hints and tips
You can also change the **font** style, size and colour of the
WordArt.

7 Now click somewhere else on the page. This will change the menus at the top back to the normal Publisher menus.

23.4 Adding text frames

The details about the play are contained within a number of text boxes. You will need to add these boxes roughly in the positions shown and then add the text to them.

To add a text box:

1 Click on the text frame tool on the **toolbar** on the left-hand side.

2 Now position the mouse pointer on the page, left click and drag out a text box roughly to the right size, then release the mouse button.
Again, if you want to adjust the size or location afterwards, you can.

3 Now type in the text.

Hints and tips
Remember that you can use the F9 key at any point to zoom in and out.

---

4 Re-size the text frame so that the text fits neatly in it.
5 Change the font to Arial by selecting it and then selecting the Arial font from the list as shown and set the size to 14 (see picture on next page top).
6 Make sure that you can still read all of the text. Publisher will warn you if the frame is too small to fit in all of the text.

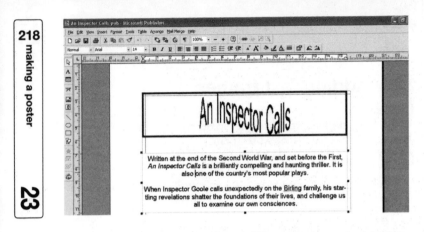

7 Now centre the text in the middle of the frame by **highlighting** it and clicking on the 'centre alignment' icon on the toolbar.

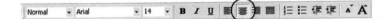

8 Add any further text frames that you need and then type the text into them. In this example, there are three more text frames: one for the actors, one for the dates and times, and one for the prices. Notice that:

- The text frames containing information on dates and times and the prices have been formatted to Arial font size 14 and the text has been centred.
- The text frames containing the information on actors is formatted to Arial font size 14.

Obviously you can choose any font styles and sizes you like in your posters. Bear in mind that this is likely to be stuck up on a notice board somewhere so needs to have a big enough font size for people to read.

23.5 Adding images

There are two images used in this example. One is a **ClipArt** image and the other is a copyright free image found on the **Internet**.

The process of adding images is similar to adding text in that you must first add the frames. To add the ClipArt image:

1 Select the 'Clip gallery tool' icon from the toolbar on the left-hand side.

2 Drag out a box in the correct place on the page.
3 The ClipArt library will now open and you can **search** or **browse** for a suitable image. This image was found by selecting the 'Entertainment' category.

Hints and tips
The contents of the ClipArt library can vary from computer to computer depending on what version of Publisher you have. This exact image might not be available on your computer.

To add the photograph:

1 Select the 'Picture frame tool' icon from the toolbar on the left.

2 Drag out a frame into the correct position.
3 Now go onto the Internet and find a suitable image. Alternatively, if you already have an image yourself, you can use the 'Insert', 'Picture' and 'From File' options.

4 When you have found the image, right click on it and select 'Copy'.
5 Now click in the picture frame that you have just put in, and right click and select 'Paste'.
The image will now be pasted into the frame and you can re-size it if necessary.

23.6 Adjusting the layout

The final poster should now be looking something like the one shown earlier. Remember that you can make changes to any part at any time. You can:

- move frames
- re-size frames
- add and remove text from frames
- delete complete frames and add new ones
- change the font style, size and colour . . .

. . . and you already know how to do all of these things!

Another useful feature is that you can put borders around each individual frame. To put a border around any of the frames:

1 Right click on the frame.
2 Select 'Change Frame'.
3 Select 'Line/border style' and choose which style of line you would like.

You can use this same method to add 'fill' colours to frames as well. This means that they will have a background colour in the frame:

1 Right click on the frame.
2 Select 'Change Frame'.
3 Select 'Fill Color'.
4 A small number of colours are shown. These will include any colours currently being used in the publication.
5 Select 'More Colors'. You can now choose any colour you like by clicking somewhere in the spectrum of colours being shown.
6 Click 'OK' when you have chosen.
Use of colour will make your poster stand out more, but bear in mind that it will use up your ink cartridges quite quickly.

Hints and tips

Also remember that many of the options that you have used in Word and PowerPoint® are also available in Publisher so don't be afraid to experiment a bit.

When you have finished, make sure you save you work. Publisher will have prompted you to save by now anyway. Then you can click on the cross to close Publisher.

Summary

In this chapter we have discussed:

- How to use a blank publication to start from scratch in Publisher
- How to work with different types of frame
- How to add text, WordArt, ClipArt and photographs
- How to add borders and fill colours to frames

24

keeping track of your personal finances

In this chapter you will learn:

- the basics of Microsoft® Excel spreadsheet software
- how to type text and numbers into cells
- how to carry out automatic calculations
- how to update your spreadsheets
- how to print spreadsheets

24.1 Introduction

Spreadsheet software is designed specifically to work with numbers. It can be used for any job where you need to carry out calculations of figures. It is much more than a calculator though, as you can set up spreadsheets that will work automatically. In this example, we will create a spreadsheet of personal finances for the month. Once it has been set up, all you have to do next month is update the figures, and the whole thing updates automatically.

24.2 Spreadsheet basics

The easiest way to understand a spreadsheet is to look at one.

Double click on 'Microsoft Excel' from your **desktop,** or if you don't have a link on your desktop, click on 'Start', 'All Programs' and find it in the list.

Excel® will open and you will see this screen:

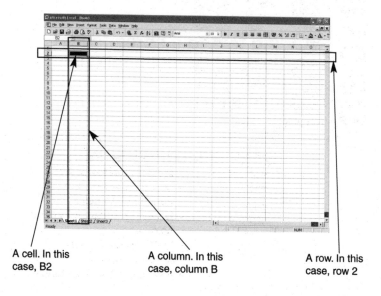

A cell. In this case, B2

A column. In this case, column B

A row. In this case, row 2

As you can see, you are faced with a large grid made up of
columns and **rows**. Across the top of the grid there are letters (for
each column) and down the left-hand side, there are numbers (for
each row). Each small box in the grid is called a **cell**. Each cell
can be referenced using the letters and numbers. For example, B2
is the cell reference where column B and row 2 meet. It is shown
in black on the diagram.

Hints and tips
Think of the letters and numbers like coordinates on a map. If you
have ever played the game Battleships, it is exactly the same principle being used here.

There are only three things that you can type into each cell:

- Text: normal text can be typed in so that you can add titles
  and labels e.g. 'Finances for June'.
- Numbers: the numbers that you want to calculate e.g. all of
  your monthly expenses.
- Formulae: these are calculations e.g. adding up all of your
  monthly expenses to get a total.

We are now going to work through a typical example setting up
a spreadsheet that records all the money coming in and all the
money going out of a typical household for the period of a month.

24.3 Adding text to a spreadsheet

First, we need to put a clear title on the spreadsheet:

1 Click in cell A1.
2 Type 'Monthly Budget' as shown on the screen below.
   Notice how the title goes across cells A1 and B1. This does
   not matter at this stage.

3 In cell A3, type 'Outgoings'. We are going to use column A to list all of the items that you have to pay for every month (e.g. gas bills, food bills, etc.).

4 Click in cell A4. Now type the first of your outgoings (e.g. Gas).

5 Click in cell A5 and type the next outgoing (e.g. Electricity).

6 Keep going until you have listed all of your outgoings. Your spreadsheet will now look something like this:

Hints and tips

Row 2 has been left blank just to make the spreadsheet easier to read. You can lay out your spreadsheet however you like.

24.4 Making the columns wider

Some of the descriptions are too wide to fit in the cells and they are taking up column A and column B. Column A needs to be wide enough to fit in the longest title. To do this, you can **drag** the column out using the mouse:

1 Move the **mouse pointer** to in between the letters A and B as shown (on the next page).
The mouse pointer will change to a line with two arrows pointing in different directions. ⟷

2 When the mouse pointer changes, hold down the left mouse button and move the mouse to the right. You will see that the column gets wider.

3 Widen the column until it is wide enough to include the longest description in your list. Then let go of the left button.

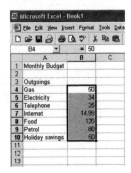

Hints and tips

It might be a bit tricky to master the mouse movement when widening columns.

24.5 Adding numbers to a spreadsheet

We are now going to use column B to type in the numbers. In this case, it will be the value in pounds of each item.

1 Click in cell B4 and type 50. Don't worry about the pound signs just yet.

2 Now complete the rest of column B typing in all the values. As this will be pounds and pence, you can type in values such as 52.34 if you want to be precise.

24.6 Formatting numbers to currency

All of the values in column B need to be shown as pounds and pence. To do this:

1 Select all of the cells from B3 to B10. You do this by positioning the mouse pointer in cell B3 and holding down the left mouse button. Then move the mouse down until you get to cell B10 and let go of the mouse button. You will see the cells go grey showing you that you are selecting them.

2 With the cells selected, click on 'Format' from the **menu** options across the top of the screen.

3 Select 'Cells' and then select 'Currency' from the list. It is set to UK pounds so assuming that is what you want, click on 'OK'.

You will see that all of the values in column B are now showing a pounds and pence.

24.7 Using formulae (sums)

The next step is to total up all of the outgoings for the month.

1 Click in cell A11 and type 'Total outgoings'.
So far we have typed text and numbers. We now need to use a formula to add up all of the outgoings.

2 Click in cell B11.

3 Click on the **autosum** Σ **icon** on the **toolbar** at the top of the screen. Excel® assumes that you want to add up all the values in column B and it will put these into a sum for you. In this case, the sum it does is:

=SUM(B4:B10)

This means that it will sum (add up) all of the values in the cells from B4 to B10 as shown.

4 Press ENTER. It will now show the total value in cell B11.

The next step is to add any further text, numbers or formulae that are needed. In this case, it means putting in all of the money coming in each month. You could do this further down column A, or use the other columns. In this example, we have used columns D and E:

Hints and tips
There are hundreds of columns and thousands of rows so you are never going to run out. To keep **scrolling** to a minimum, try to design your spreadsheets so that they fit onto one screen full.

1   Type 'Income' into cell D3 as shown:

You will need to widen column D and **format** column E to Currency as previously described.

2   In cell D11, type 'Total Income' as shown. It has been put here so that it is in the same row as the Total outgoings.

3   Click in E11 and click on the autosum button.
    Excel® has guessed at which cells you want to add up, but this time, it has got it wrong.

4   Click in cell E11 and change the formula so that it reads =SUM(E4:E6). To do this, point the mouse between the E and the 11 and click. Delete the 11 and put 6 instead.

5   Press ENTER.
    The Total income value is now shown.
    The final stage is to do a calculation to see how much money you have left each month.

6   In cell A13, type 'Money left'.

7   In cell B13, type '=E11-B11'
    This will take the value in B11 (Total outgoings) away from the value in E11 (Total income) to show you the money you have left. In this case, it is £426.01.

24.8 Saving your spreadsheet

At this stage, you are probably thinking that you could have done all of this much quicker on a calculator – and you might be right. However, the beauty of spreadsheets is that once you have set one up, you can use it over and over again. All you need to do next month is change the figures, and all of the calculations will update automatically.

To do this:

1 Click on 'File' and 'Save' from the menu bar at the top, or click on the 'Save icon'. 🖫
2 The **file** save window is now displayed and it is set up to put things into the **folder** called My documents. You can change to a different folder if you have set one up, or save it here.
3 Where it says 'File Name' at the bottom, type in 'June Finances'.

This will save the file as June Finances in the My Documents folder. This is where it will be if you want to open it again at a later stage. You can safely close the file now.

24.9 Updating a spreadsheet

Let's now assume a month has passed and we want to do our finances for July.

1 Open the June Finances file (it may already be open).
2 In cells B4 to B10 you can change the outgoings for July. In cells E4 to E6, you can change the income figures for July.

It is important that you do *not* change the values in any cell where you have done a formula, as these do not need changing.

For example, let's say that the food bill went up this month to £150:

3 Click in cell B8 and type in '150'.
Now look in cells B11, E11 and B13 where all the totals are calculated. They have changed automatically as a result of the change you made in cell B8.

Hints and tips
This is where a spreadsheet can really save you time as once you have set them up, you can change the figures and all of the totals will re-calculate automatically.

You now need to save this file with a new name:

1 Click on 'File' from the menu options.
2 Click on 'Save As'.
This will save the file with a new name.
As before, the standard folder for saving your work is called My Documents.

3   Where it says 'File Name' at the bottom, type in 'July Finances'. This means that the June Finances file will still be there in case you ever need it again and you will have a new file called July Finances.

You can repeat this process each month creating a whole archive of files.

24.10 Making spreadsheets look attractive

Spreadsheets are mainly used for (boring) financial stuff and it is usually sufficient for them to be fairly plain in terms of the layout. In the example above, we left a row spare and lined up our totals to make it a bit easier to read. Apart from that, the layout was a bit dull.

There are things that you can do to liven up spreadsheets a bit. You can:

- Add colour to the text, the cell backgrounds and borders.
- Change **font** styles and sizes.
- Add borders around cells.

The process for doing any of these things is quite similar so you might want to experiment with them a bit.

Start by selecting the cells that you want to change. For example, to change the font in all the cells on the June Finances spreadsheet:

1   Select all of the cells from A1 to F13. Do this by clicking in cell A1 and holding down the left mouse button while moving it across to F13. When you get to F13, release the left mouse button.
    Now that the cells are selected:
2   Select 'Format' from the menu at the top.
3   Select 'Cells'.
4   Click on the 'Font' tab. You can now change the font size and style.
5   Click on 'OK' when complete.

To apply changes to specific cells, click on the individual cell rather than selecting a range of cells. For example, to **highlight** the title in blue:

1   Click on cell A1.
2   Click on the 'Font color' icon.

3 Select one of the blues and the colour of the text in cell A1 will change to blue.

The other options here are the cell fill colour which colours

 in, the cell and the border option, which will put a border around cells to make them stand out.

All of these options work in the same way. The **bold** and *italic* options can also be applied in exactly the same way as in Word. Select the cell or range of cells that you want to change, and then click on the option that you want to apply.

This final image shows a more attractive spreadsheet that has been created simply by using bold text and borders to highlight the important cells, and increasing the font size of the titles.

	A	B	C	D	E	F
1	**Monthly Budget**					
2						
3	**Outgoings**			**Income**		
4	Gas	£50.00		Pension	£300.00	
5	Electricity	£34.00		Interest on saving	£100.00	
6	Telephone	£25.00		Part-time job	£400.00	
7	Internet	£14.99				
8	Food	£120.00				
9	Petrol	£80.00				
10	Holiday savings	£50.00				
11	**Total outgoings**	£373.99		**Total Income**	£800.00	
12						
13	**Money left**	£426.01				
14						
15						
16						
17						

Microsoft Excel - June finances.xls

Summary

In this chapter we have discussed:

- How to use a spreadsheet
- How to add text, numbers and formulae
- How to save and update a spreadsheet
- How to improve the appearance of a spreadsheet

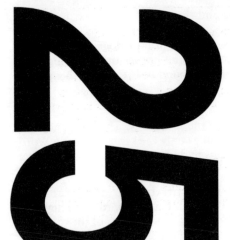

25 keeping track of your investments

In this chapter you will learn:

- how to calculate values using percentages in Excel®
- how to type in formulae
- how to copy and paste formulae between cells
- how to wrap text within a cell
- how to create graphs

Aim of this chapter

The aim of this chapter is to help you to keep track of your personal investments using spreadsheet software. It will show you how to type in all of your investments (savings or shares, for example) and how to track the value of these investments and what returns you can expect on them each month. It is assumed that you have worked through Chapter 24 and that you are familiar with the basics of spreadsheets.

25.1 Introduction

If you have personal savings accounts, bonds or shares, then you will know the value of these investments. Each month you might want to calculate how much money you can expect to receive in interest or dividends. You might also want to track the total value of your shares if you were considering selling them.

This chapter will show you how to set up a **spreadsheet** to do this and show you how to produce a graph so that you visualize the return on your investment.

25.2 Setting up the spreadsheet

You might want to type in your own figures for your own investments, or you can work through the example provided here.

1 Open the Excel® **software** by double clicking on the **icon** from the **desktop,** or from the Start **menu.**
2 You are then presented with an empty 'worksheet' made up of many **cells.**
3 In cell A1, type in a title, for example: My Investments.

4   List your investments in **column** A or copy the example below.
    Notice that we have split out the savings from the shares.

Hints and tips

If you have lots of savings accounts or shares, you might want to create a separate spreadsheet for each. Also, we have done a monthly spreadsheet. You might want to do yours over a longer period.

We are now going to add some column headings for the information that we need to know about each investment.

1   In cell B3, type 'Amount saved'.
2   In cell C3, type 'Interest rate'.
3   In cell D3, type 'Interest gained'.

You will need to widen each column so that the words fit in the cells. Your spreadsheet should now look like this.

The column headings we need for the shares are different:

4   In cell B7, type 'Number of shares'.
5   In cell C7, type 'Price paid per share'.
6   In cell D7, type 'Current price per share'.
7   In cell E7, type 'Total paid'.
8   In cell E8, type 'Total value now'.

Again you will need to widen the columns to get the titles in.

Hints and tips

You don't have to stick with these headings. You can create your own. The meaning of each column will become clear when the numbers are added later.

25.3 Wrapping text

When you type into **word processing** software such as Word, you get to the end of the line and the **cursor** automatically moves to the start of the next line. This is called **wrapping**. We can use wrapping in Excel® too. You might have noticed that the columns are getting quite wide so that the text fits in. Using text wrapping, we can split the text over more than one line in each cell.

1 Select cells A7 to F7 by doing a left click and hold on cell A7 and then **dragging** the **mouse pointer** to F7 and letting go.
2 Click on 'Format' from the menu options at the top.
3 Click on 'Cells' and then on 'Alignment'. The following screen is displayed.

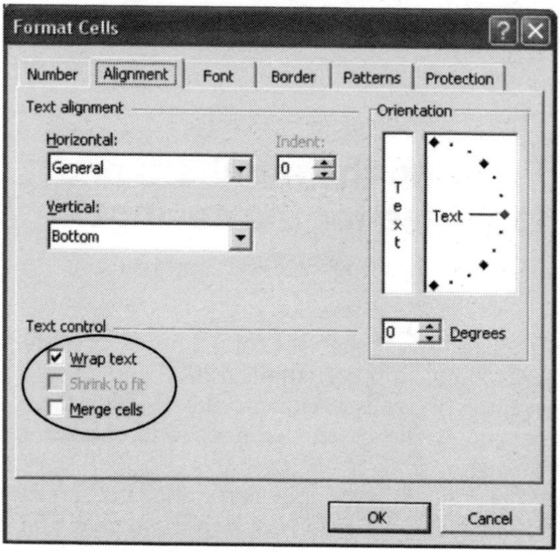

4 Click on the box that reads 'Wrap text' as shown.
5 Click on 'OK'.
6 Now make the columns narrower. As you do this, you will see that the text is wrapping over two lines as shown (see next page).

	A	B	C	D	E	F	G
1	My Investments						
2							
3	Savings	Amount saved	Interest rate	Interest gained			
4	Savings Account 1	50000	5%	208.3333333			
5	Savings Account 2	23000	4.75%				
6							
7	Shares	Number of shares	Price per share paid	Current price per share	Total paid	Total value now	
8	Company 1	6000	2.5	2.53			
9	Company 2	1000	4	4.5			
10	Company 3	300	1.5	1.25			
11	Company 4	200	1.32				
12							
13							
14							
15							
16							
17							

25.4 Entering the numbers and formulae for the savings

Now that all the headings are set up, you can type in the values.

1 In cells B4 and B5, type in the total amount of money in each savings account, in this example 50000 and 23000.
2 Format these two cells to currency by selecting them, clicking on 'Format', 'Cells', then 'Number' and choose 'Currency' from the list.
3 In cells C4 and C5, type in the percentage interest rate, in this case 5% and 4.75%. It is very important that you type the percentage (%) sign (SHIFT and 5) so that Excel® knows this is a percentage.
4 In cell B4, a formula is needed to work out how much interest has been gained. This will be B4 × C4. Because we are doing monthly figures, it also needs to be divided by 12 as the interest rate is annual. In cell B4, type =B4*C4/12

The multiply sign is the asterisk (*). There is a key for it on the right-hand side of your keyboard or you can use SHIFT and 8. The divide key is a slash. It is located towards the bottom right-hand side of the letters on the keyboard.

5 The amount of interest earned is now displayed. Format this to currency in the usual way. This will add the £ sign and limit the number to two decimal places.

6 Rather than typing the formula again in D5, you can **copy** the formula from D4 to D5. To do this, right click on cell D4 and select 'Copy'. Then click on cell D5 and right click and select 'Paste'.

The formula is copied and Excel® cleverly changes it so that it is =B5*C5/12. Also, because the format of the cell was currency, it copies the format into the new cell.

25.5 Entering the numbers and formulae for the shares

The numbers and formulae needed to calculate how much the shares are worth is different.

First, you need to enter the numbers as shown in the diagram on next page.

1 In cells B8 to B11, type in the number of shares held in each company. In this example: B8 is 5000, B9 is 1000, B10 is 300 and B11 is 200.

	A	B	C	D	E	F	G
1	My Investments						
2							
3	Savings	Amount saved	Interest rate	Interest gained			
4	Savings Account 1	£50,000.00	5%	£208.33			
5	Savings Account 2	£23,000.00	4.75%	£91.04			
6							
7	Shares	Number of shares	Price per share paid	Current price per share	Total paid	Total value now	
8	Company 1	5000	£2.50	£2.53			
9	Company 2	1000	£4.00	£4.50			
10	Company 3	300	£1.50	£1.25			
11	Company 4	200	£1.32	£1.43			
12							
13							

2 In cells C8 to C11, type in the amount that was paid for each individual share. In this example: C8 is £2.50, C9 is £4.00, C10 is £1.50 and C11 is £1.32.

3 In cells D8 to D11, type in the current price of each share. In

this example: D8 is £2.53, D9 is £4.50, D10 is £1.25 ad D11 is £1.43.

Columns E and F need formulae in them as they can be calculated from the other columns.

4 In cell E8, type =B8*C8. This is the total amount spent on shares in Company 1. Format this to currency in the usual way.
5 In cell F8, type =D8*D8. This is the total amount that the shares would be worth if you sold them now. Format this to currency in the usual way.

Hints and tips
You can go on forever with spreadsheets. For example, you could add another formula in column G to work out the difference between columns E and F, or you could add subtotals in row 12.

25.6 Copying formulae across cells

There are just a few cells left to fill in. You could type in the formula as described previously. However, as the formulae needed are all basically the same, you can copy the existing formulae into the blank cells. For example, the formulae needed in cells E9 to E11 are basically the same as the one used in cell E8. The formulae needed in cells F9 to F11 are basically the same as the one used in cell F8.

Let's start by copying the formula into E9 to E11:

1 Click in cell E8.
2 Move the mouse pointer into the bottom right-hand corner of cell E8 until the mouse pointer changes to a small black cross. ✚

urrent price er share	Total paid	Total value now
£2.53	£12,500.00	£12,650.0
£4.50		

3 Now hold down the left button on the mouse and move the mouse down so that you are selecting cells E9, E10 and E11.
4 Then let go of the left mouse button.
   The formula has now been copied down into these cells and Excel® has automatically changed it so that it refers to the correct cell references.

5 You now need to do exactly the same thing copying the formula in F8 to cells F9, F10 and F11.

Your spreadsheet is now complete.

6 Save it and give it a sensible name, for example: My Investments.

Remember that you can now come back and change this spreadsheet at any time. For example, if interest rates change, or if share prices change, you can type in the new values and the spreadsheet will recalculate all your figures automatically.

25.7 Creating a graph

A graph or chart is a visual way of looking at data. It can be easier to look at a graph and understand what is happening rather than looking at rows and rows of numbers.

Hints and tips

Like other things in Excel®, once you have set up your graph, it will change automatically if any of the numbers change.

First you need to decide what you want to create a graph of. A useful graph in this example would be to plot the 'Total paid' and 'Total value now' values to see whether each company has made you any money or not.

The first step is to select the cells that you want to plot. As well as selecting the cells, you also need to select the text, as Excel® is clever enough to put these onto the graph for you as axes labels.

1 Select cells A7 to A11 by clicking and holding on A7 and then dragging the mouse down to A11.
2 Now hold down the CTRL key and select cells E7 to F11 in exactly the same way. You will notice that A7 to A11 remain selected and that all the cells from E7 to F11 are also selected.

Holding down the CTRL key allows you to select groups of cells that are not next to each other in the spreadsheet. This is very useful when you just want to graph certain values, as in this case.

---

3 Now click on the 'Chart Wizard' icon on the **toolbar**.
The **wizard** will take you through several screens prompting you for choices about how you want your graph to look.

Chart Wizard - Step 1 of 4 - Chart Type

Standard Types | Custom Types

Chart type:

- Column
- Bar
- Line
- Pie
- XY (Scatter)
- Area
- Doughnut
- Radar
- Surface
- Bubble
- Stock

Chart sub-type:

Clustered Column. Compares values across categories.

Press and Hold to View Sample

Cancel | < Back | Next > | Finish

4   Click on 'Next'. This selects a column chart.

Chart Wizard - Step 3 of 4 - Chart Options

Titles | Axes | Gridlines | Legend | Data Labels | Data Table

Chart title:
show value of my shares

Category (X) axis:
Company Name

Value (Y) axis:
Value of shares

Second category (X) axis:

Second value (Y) axis:

Graph to show value of my shares

Cancel | < Back | Next > | Finish

5   A **preview** of what the chart will look like is then displayed. Click 'Next'.

6   You are now prompted to enter a Chart title and the x and y
    axes labels.

    • Type 'Chart to show value of my shares' as the chart title.
    • Type 'Company Name' as the x axis label.
    • Type 'Value of shares' as the y axis label.

7   Click 'Next'.
8   Click 'Finish'.
    The graph is now shown in your spreadsheet. You can click
    on it and drag it around, putting it wherever you want on the
    page. You can also re-size it by clicking on one of the corners
    and dragging to a larger or smaller size.
9   In this case, drag the graph just below all of the figures as
    there is room for both with the graph at the current size.
10 Save your **file** again.

If you change any of the values for the shares in the cells, you will
notice that the graph updates itself automatically.

Summary

In this chapter we have discussed:
• How to calculate percentages
• How to carry out more complex formulae
• How to copy formulae from one cell to another
• How to wrap text within a cell
• How to create graphs

26 keeping lists of names and addresses

In this chapter you will learn:

- how to use Microsoft®
  Access database software
- how to set up a database of
  names and addresses
- how to add, change and
  remove information in a
  database
- how to search for information
  stored in a database
- how to sort a database
- how to print names and
  addresses onto labels

> **Aims of this chapter**
> This chapter will introduce you to database software. It will show you how to set it up to store useful information and then how you can use the database to search quickly for that information.

26.1 Introduction

A **database** is a collection of related information. For example, your doctor's surgery will have a database that lists all of the patients and details about them; every time you receive a piece of junk mail through the post, it is because you are on a database somewhere.

Databases can be useful for personal use as well. One of the common uses is to set up a database of all of the people in your address/phone book. In this sense, a database is an electronic version of your address book. If you are involved in running a club or society, a database could be really useful for storing contact details of all the members and other useful information, such as whether they have paid their subs!

Databases are made up of fields and records. A **field** is one piece of information that is stored on the database. For example, on a doctor's surgery database the fields might be patient name, name of their doctor, date of last appointment, drugs prescribed, etc. A **record** is a collection of fields for one person. For example, your medical record is all of the information about you.

If you have worked through the chapters on **spreadsheets**, it is easiest to think of fields as **columns** and records as **rows**.

26.2 Getting started

The most common database **software** for home computer users (and for many businesses too) is Microsoft® Access. Access is a bit different from the other software that we have looked at so far in this book. There are two stages to using Access. The first is to set up the database and the second is to add all of the information.

First, you need to decide what information you want to store. The example used in this chapter will be a database of contact details for friends and families (i.e. your address book). You have to break down each piece of information that you want to store. Each different piece of information is called a field. In this case, we need the following fields:

Title (Mr, Mrs, Ms, Miss, Dr, etc.)
First Name
Last Name
Address
Postcode
Phone Number
Mobile Number
Email Address

Hints and tips
Breaking a database into fields makes it much easier to search the database later on.

---

1 Open Access either by double clicking on it from the **desktop**, or by clicking on 'Start', 'All Programs' and then finding it in the list.
2 Depending on what version you are using, the next screen looks different. However, you need to find the option for 'Blank Database' and select it.
3 You are then asked to save your database (even though you haven't actually made it yet!). This will be saved into the My Documents **folder**. Where it says 'File Name', type 'My addresses' and click 'Create'.
4 Access will now open and you will see a screen like this:

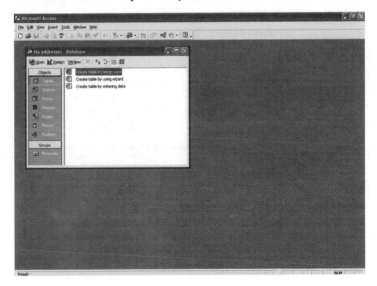

5 Double click on the first option (**highlighted** in blue) that reads: 'Create table in design view.'

The screen will then look like this.

A 'table' is where you store all of the information that you want in your database.

First, you must tell it what fields you want to use:

1 The first column is for the 'Field Name', so click in the first box and type 'Title'.
2 Now click in the next box down and type 'First Name'.
You will notice that the second column called 'Data Type' is being filled in automatically, which is fine for now.
3 Continue like this until you have typed in all of the fields that we identified earlier. Your list should look like this when complete.

26.3 Setting the correct data types

The **data types** are quite important. They tell Access how to handle the information that you are going to type in. Text is the most common data type and, as the name suggests, you use it whenever you want to type in letters. You can also use it to type in numbers. This might seem a bit odd, but if you think about the typical address, it might be something like 12 Acacia Avenue. This is actually a mixture of letters and numbers.

Hints and tips
The text data type is sometimes called 'alphanumeric', which means that you can type alphabetic characters and numbers.

In fact, all of our fields do need to be set to text. It might seem odd to set Phone Number and Mobile Number to text but you need to do this so that you can add brackets and spaces if you want to. Another reason is that if you set them to number, Access will remove the leading zero at the beginning of a number, for example 01673 343434 becomes 1673 343434, which is really annoying.

There is one other useful data type that we will use and this is called the **lookup wizard**. By now, you have probably filled in a few forms on the computer, usually on the **Internet**. Often when you are filling in a form, rather than having to type in information, you are given a choice from a list. In Access, creating a list like this is called the lookup wizard.

It would be useful to set up the Title field as a list as there are only a few choices e.g. Mr, Mrs, etc. This way, when you are typing the names and addresses, rather than having to type Mr or Mrs, you just choose from the list.

To set this up:

1 Click in the data type box that is to the right of the Title as shown.

When you click in this box, you will see a small arrow in the right-hand side of the box.

2 Click on the arrow.
3 Select 'Lookup Wizard' from this list.
4 On the next screen, select the 'I will type in the values that I want' button.

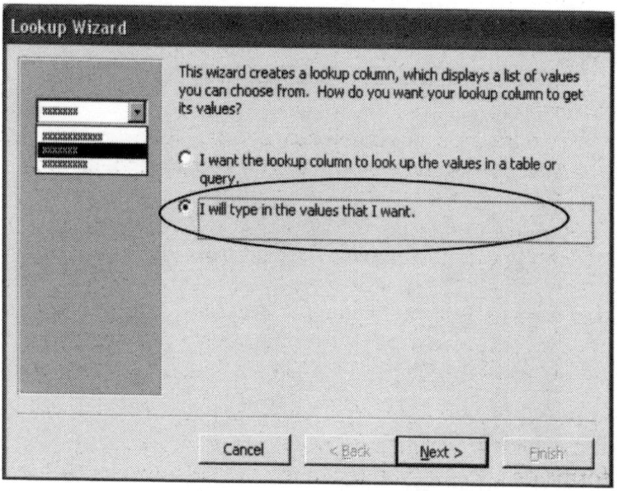

5 Click 'Next'.
6 In 'Col1', type the list of titles that you want to be available to you later on, as shown.

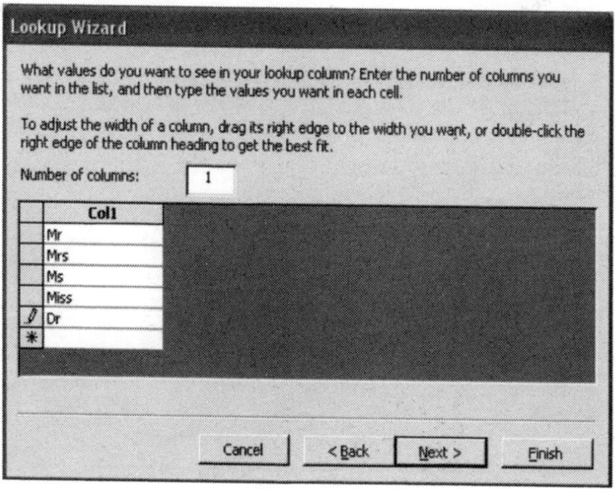

7   Click 'Next'.
8   Click 'Finish'.

It is not obvious that this has worked, but don't worry, you will
see later on where the list appears.

You now need to save these changes:

1   Click on the 'Save' **icon** on the **toolbar**.

2   Name the table: My addresses.
3   You then get a message about a 'primary key'. You can select
    'No' on this.
4   Now close this window by clicking on the cross. Make sure that
    you close this window, rather than the whole database as shown.

26.4 Typing in the names and addresses

The first stage of the process is now complete. Your database is all set up and ready to go. You now need to type in all of the information.

1 Select 'My addresses'.

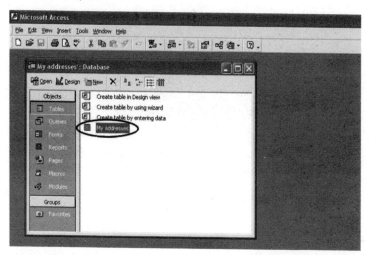

The database will now open in what is called 'View' mode. This looks a bit like a spreadsheet and works in much the same way. You can now type in the details in the relevant columns. Start with the first person:

2 Click on the little arrow in the first row of the Title column.

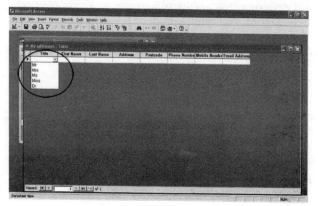

The list that we made earlier is displayed and you can choose the appropriate title by clicking on it.

3 Click in the First Name **cell** and type in the person's first name.

4 Complete the first row as per the example shown.

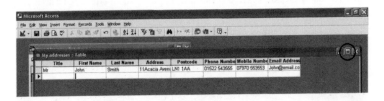

You will notice that some of the columns are not wide enough to display all of the information that you have typed into them. There are two things you can do about this. The first is to widen the columns in the same way that you do in Excel®. That is, you move the **mouse pointer** to the gap between the field names, click and hold and then **drag** the mouse to make the columns wider, or narrower.

5 Take some time to ensure that the columns are the correct width.

The second is to 'maximize' the window so that it is full screen. To do this:

6 Click on the 'maximize' button as shown in the diagram at step 4.

The example below shows a database table on full screen, with the column widths adjusted to fill the page. A few dummy records have been filled in to show you how it will look.

7 You now need to spend some time working through your address book and typing in all of the details.

Title	First Name	Last Name	Address	Postcode	Phone Number	Mobile Number	Email Address
Mr	John	Smith	11 Acacia Avenue, Lincoln	LN1 1AA	01522 543555	07970 563553	John@email.com
Mrs	Mary	Jones	42a High Street, Buttleborough, Derbyshire	DE43 5TS	01423 845464		
Dr	Raj	Sanghera	Highview Surgery, Main Road, Kettering	NN34 5TT	04536 125136		surgery@highview.co.uk
Ms	Emily	Lui	The Lodge, Beaumanor Estate, Leicester	LE34 433	01534 645464	07956 746574	

26.5 Searching for information

Once you have typed in all of the information, your database is now ready to use. The most likely use for this database is to be able to find someone's details as quickly as possible. You might have lots of records, in which case you don't want to have to scan through them all to find what you want. This is where a database is useful as you can get it to do the searching for you.

You can **search** in any of the fields. For example, if you wanted to find people called Smith, you would search in the Last Name. To do this:

1 Click in one of the 'Last Name' records in the table. It does not matter whose record you click on as long as you click on one of the last names.

2 Click on the 'Find' icon in the toolbar as shown.

3 You are now prompted to type in what you are searching for. Type 'Smith' as shown.

4 Click on the 'Find Next' button.
5 It will quickly search through the records and find the first Smith, highlighting it in black.
   If this is not the Smith you want, click 'Find Next' and it will go to the next one.

You can use this same method to find anything. The trick is to click on the table in the field that you want to search before clicking the 'Find' button.

This example database had only four records, which is a bit pathetic really. If you had only four names and addresses to enter it would not really be worth making a database in the first place. The real power of databases comes when you have got tens or even hundreds of different records to search through.

26.6 Sorting information into a particular order

In this database, it would be useful to **sort** the database in alphabetical order based on last name. It might be that if you have copied the information from your address book that it is already in alphabetical order. To make sure that it is in alphabetical order:

1 Click on the column heading 'Last Name'. When you do this, the whole column is highlighted in black.

2 Click on the 'Sort' icon in the toolbar as shown.

All of the records will be re-ordered in ascending alphabetical order. This will make it much easier to find the records you are looking for.

26.7 Editing (changing) the database

Information held on your database is likely to change. People might move house, or change their phone numbers or even join the Internet revolution and get themselves an email address!

If this happens, you simply over-type the old information with the new information. For example, if John Smith moved house to 54 The Ridings, Lincoln, you would simply click where the current address is, delete the old address and type in the new one.

To delete a whole record:

1 Find the record you want to delete.
2 Click on the number of the record on the left-hand side. This will highlight the whole row in black.
3 Right click and select 'Delete Record'. There is a final warning that you are about to delete the entire row. Click 'Yes'.

26.8 Printing name and address labels

You may want to print your names and address onto sticky labels, which you can then stick on envelopes. This is particularly useful for sending out cards at Christmas, or if you are involved with a club or society. To do this, you will need to use what is called **mail merge**. This is actually available in Word, but will use the database that you have set up in Access. We will use the 'My addresses' database set up earlier in this chapter.

1 Open Word.
2 Select 'Tools' from the menu bar at the top.
3 Select 'Mail Merge'.
   You will now see the Mail Merge screen that looks like this:

Mail Merge Helper

Use this checklist to set up a mail merge. Begin by choosing the Create button.

1 Main document
   Create ▾

2 Data source
   Get Data ▾

3 Merge the data with the document
   Merge...

Cancel

4 Select 'Create'.
5 Select 'Mailing Labels'.
6 Select 'Active Window'.
7 Now select 'Get Data' and 'Open Data Source'.
  You now need to tell it to get the data from your 'My addresses' database.
8 Click on 'My Documents'.
  You now need to tell it to look for Access files.
9 Click on the 'Files of type' drop down arrow as shown:

10 Select 'MS Access Databases' from this list.
11 Find the 'My addresses' database and click on it.
12 Click on 'OK'.
  You will now be asked to set up the main document.
13 Click on 'Set Up Main Document'.

At this stage you will need to know what type of labels you will be using. This should be written on the packaging of the labels.

Hints and tips
There are hundreds of different labels to choose from. Make sure you get the right size and the ones that work in your printer.

---

14 Select the appropriate label type from this list shown.

You now need to tell it what you want on the labels (i.e. the name and address details).

The following screen will be displayed:

```
┌─────────────────────────────────────────────────────────────┐
│  Create Labels                                      [?][X]    │
├─────────────────────────────────────────────────────────────┤
│                                                               │
│  ┌─────────────────────────────────────────────────────────┐ │
│  │ Choose the Insert Merge Field button to insert merge    │ │
│  │ fields into the sample label.  You can edit and format   │ │
│  │ the merge fields and text in the Sample Label box.       │ │
│  └─────────────────────────────────────────────────────────┘ │
│                                                               │
│     ┌─────────────────────────────┐                          │
│     │   Insert Merge Field  ▼     │                          │
│     └─────────────────────────────┘                          │
│  Sample label:                                                │
│  ┌───────────────────────────────────────────────────────┐▲  │
│  │                                                       │   │
│  │                                                       │   │
│  │                                                       │   │
│  │                                                       │   │
│  │                                                       │   │
│  └───────────────────────────────────────────────────────┘▼  │
│                                                               │
│                        ┌──────────┐      ┌──────────┐         │
│                        │    OK    │      │  Cancel  │         │
│                        └──────────┘      └──────────┘         │
└─────────────────────────────────────────────────────────────┘
```

15 Click on 'Insert Merge Field' and each of the fields that you set up earlier will be displayed.

16 Select 'Title' from the list, then press the SPACE bar, then select 'Insert Merge Field' again, select 'First Name', then press the SPACE bar, select 'Insert Merge Field, and then 'Last Name'.

This means that the names will appear with a space between them, for example Mr John Smith instead of MrJohnSmith.

17 Press ENTER and then select the 'Address'.

18 Press ENTER and then select the 'Postcode'.

19 Click 'OK'.

20 Click 'Merge' and then click 'Merge' again on the next screen. Your Word document will now display the labels in the correct format.

21 Insert the labels into the printer making sure you get them the right way up.

22 Click on 'Print'.

23 Now save the document as: Address labels.

24 You can now close Word.

Summary

In this chapter we have discussed:

- How to create a database of names and addresses
- How to add, change and remove information
- How to search and sort a database
- How to print out names and addresses onto labels

27 creating a slideshow presentation for a group

In this chapter you will learn:

- how to use Microsoft PowerPoint® software
- how to create a computer-based slideshow
- how to add text, images and photographs to your slideshow
- how to run a slideshow

Aim of this chapter

This chapter will show you how to create a slideshow presentation on the computer. A slideshow presentation is a series of slides or screens with information on them. You might want to put one together if you have to present information to a group of people. For example, you might want to show your holiday photographs in this way. Perhaps you are the member of a club or society and need to do a presentation to them. This chapter will show you how to do this.

Hints and tips

Slideshow presentation is a bit of a mouthful so they will be called either presentations or slideshows. Both words mean the same thing.

27.1 Introduction

Slideshows can be used anytime you want to present information to people. If you think about the holiday photographs example above, the photos are transferred onto slides and then the person projects the slides onto a screen one by one while talking about them.

A PowerPoint® slideshow is the modern equivalent of this and can be used in any situation where you want to present information to one or more people. It is possible to project computer images onto larger screens using a specialized projector. These are quite expensive and it is not suggested that you go out and buy one just for personal use. However, projectors are common in schools and colleges and are becoming more common in clubs and societies so you might get the chance to use one.

Even without a projector, a slideshow can be presented on the computer screen, which is often sufficient for a smaller audience. Another option is to send people your slideshow so that they can view it on their own computer.

Hints and tips

If you are not talking people through your slideshow, you might need to put more detailed explanations in the text.

27.2 Getting started

1 Open Microsoft PowerPoint® either by double clicking on the **icon** on your **desktop,** or by going to 'Start', 'All Programs' and clicking on it in the list.
2 The first screen asks you what kind of presentation you want. Select 'Blank presentation' as shown.

You are now shown a selection of slide layouts. One slide will take up one screen-full when the slideshow is being shown. Slideshows will contain several slides. The number of slides depends on how long you want the presentation to be.

Hints and tips

If you are going to present your slides (i.e. talk about them as you show them), a rough rule of thumb is that you need approximately one slide for every three minutes of talk.

The first slide is normally an introduction slide that introduces the topic and the speaker/writer.

3   Select the slide layout in the top left-hand corner. This is a title slide.

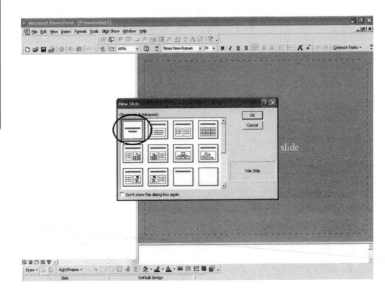

4   Click on 'OK'.

You are now presented with your first slide, which at the moment is blank.

Hints and tips
PowerPoint® works in much the same way as Word. The main difference is that you are creating a slideshow that will be shown on computer, rather than a document that will be printed out.

The blank area on the left of the screen is an outline view of your slideshow. As you fill in each slide, the text that you type will be shown in this area. This is really useful as you add more and more slides.

The main window is the slide itself and this particular slide has space for a title and a subtitle.

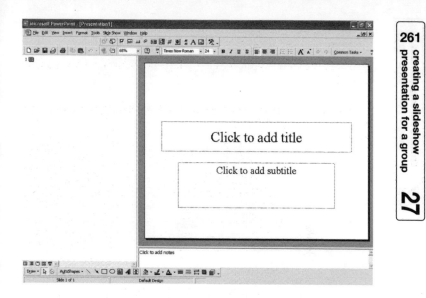

5 Click where it says 'Click to add title'. You can now type in the name of the presentation. In this example type 'Volunteer Work'.

6 Click where it says 'Click to add subtitle' and type your name in here.

The **font** size looks massive compared to sizes that you have been using in other chapters. However, this is because it is designed to be presented to a group so the font needs to be big.

Notice how the outline view on the left of the screen also shows the text that you have typed in. You can edit the slide here as well if you want to.

27.3 Adding more slides

You are now ready to add more slides:

1 Click on 'Insert' from the **menu** bar across the top.

2 The 'New Slide' window is shown again. The next slide is going to contain text with **bullet points** (see slide on next page top).

3 Select the layout shown and click 'OK'.
   This slide is a different layout, but you add text to it in the same way as the first slide.

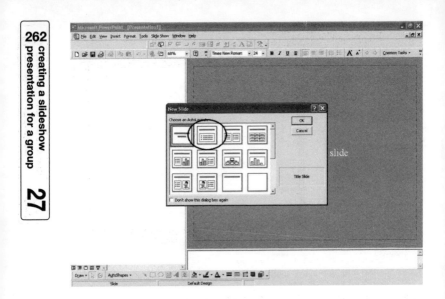

4 Click where it says 'Click to add title' and type in the title for
   this slide. In this example 'Why volunteer?'
5 Now click where it says 'Click to add text'. You can now type
   in a series of bullet points.
   The idea of bullet points is that you summarize what it is you
   are trying to say. This means that what you write should be
   short and to the point. If you are presenting the slideshow,
   you can use the bullet points as prompts to what you want to
   say.
6 Type in the first bullet point. In this example 'Giving something back'.
7 Press ENTER. You will see that the next bullet point appears
   automatically so you can type in the next point. Type
   'Helping the local community'.
8 Continue until you have made all the points you want to. In
   this example, there are five different points.

Hints and tips
The size of the font is automatic. If you type lots of bullet points,
it will automatically make the font smaller to fit it all in.

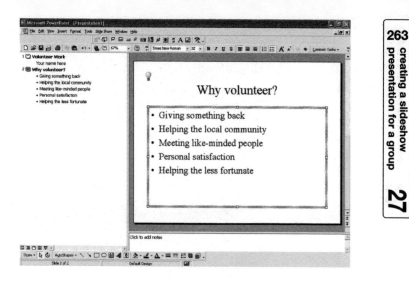

27.4 Adding ClipArt to slides

Now we will add a slide with a picture in it. **ClipArt** is a library of images, some animated and some photographs. In the next example, there will be text and an image on the slide.

1 Click on 'Insert' and 'New Slide'.
2 Select the slide layout shown in the diagram and click 'OK'.

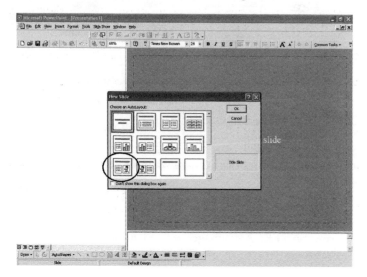

The title and text can now be added in the same way that you added them in the previous slides.

3 In this example the slide title will be 'How to volunteer'.

4 The bullet list should read:

- Go to your nearest volunteer centre
- Look in yellow pages
- Volunteer online

Next add the image.

5 Double click where it says: 'Double click to add clipart'.

6 The ClipArt library will now load.

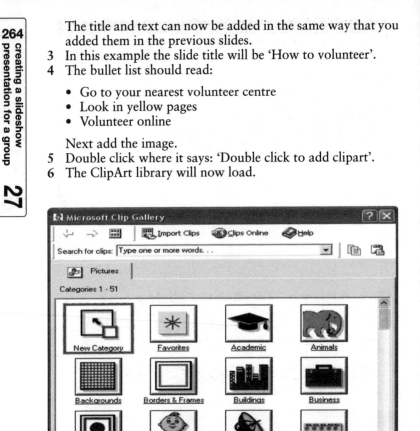

ClipArt is organized in categories. The amount of images you have depends on what version of the **software** you have. You can click on each of the categories and then **browse** through the images until you find the one you want, or you can **search** for a specific image.

For example, if we wanted a ClipArt image of a computer:

7 Where is says 'Search for clips', type in 'computer' and press ENTER. Any images related to computers are now shown.

In this case, it has found three suitable images.

8 Select the image you want, in this example the first one.

9 A small menu is displayed. Select the first option as shown. This will insert the image into the slideshow.

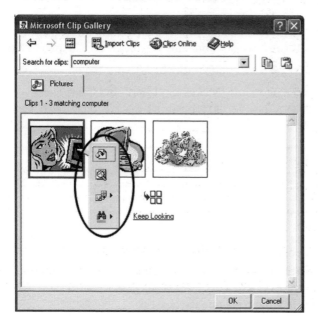

Your finished slide will now look like this.

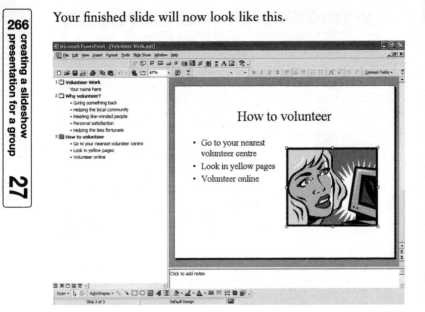

27.5 Adding photographs to slides

This section will show you how to insert a photograph. It assumes that you already have some photographs on your computer. If you have not done this yet, please see Chapters 17 to 19.

First, create a new slide into which to put the photograph:

1 Add a new slide by clicking 'Insert' and 'New Slide'.
2 Select the same layout as before, which is part text, part picture.

Hints and tips

If you were creating a slideshow that was just photographs with no text, then you could choose the blank slide layout which is the last option.

---

3 Type in a title and the bullet point text in the usual way. In this example, the title is 'John: a case study'.
4 The bullet points should read:

- John volunteered at his local centre
- He volunteers one day a week

- He helps disabled people with their gardens
- He loves being outdoors and helping people

> **Hints and tips**
> There is quite a lot of text for a smallish box here so you will see that PowerPoint® automatically reduces the font size to fit it all in.

To add a photograph:

5 Single click (*not* double click) where it says: 'Double click to add clipart'.
6 Click on 'Insert' from the menu bar at the top.
7 Select 'Picture' and 'From File'.
   The My Pictures folder is now shown. Assuming that your photograph is in this folder, find it in the list and double click on it.

The photograph will be inserted into the slide. The size of the photograph will depend on how the picture was saved – it may be the wrong size when you first insert it. If it is:

8 Click on the photograph.
9 Move the **mouse pointer** to one of the four corners until the mouse pointer changes to this shape ↘.
10 Now hold down the left mouse button and move the mouse – the photograph will re-size. When it is the size you want it, release the left mouse button.

You can also move the picture around if you need to.

> **Hints and tips**
> You can also **copy and paste** images into PowerPoint®. For example, if you found a good image on the **Internet** you could copy it from there and paste it into your slide.

27.6 Saving the slideshow

At this stage, it is worth saving the slideshow. The saving process is the same here as for all other software:

1 Click on the 'Save' icon in the **toolbar,** or select 'File' and 'Save'.
2 Give your presentation a suitable name (e.g. Volunteer Work).

27.7 Running the slideshow

When you run the slideshow, it will be shown as full-screen. This is how your audience will see it. They may be viewing it on their own computer, or you might be projecting it onto a big screen.

To view the slideshow:

1 Click on the first slide in the outline view as shown, or press F5.
2 In the bottom left-hand screen there is a little row of icons, as shown.

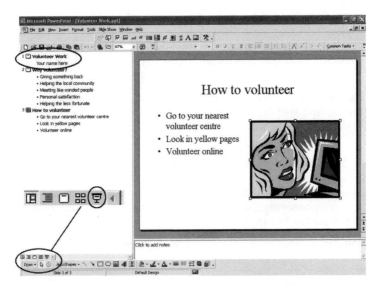

3 Select the 'Slide Show' option as shown.
  Your slideshow will now run in full screen displaying the first slide.
4 Click the mouse once. Slide 2 is now shown. Each click will move the slideshow on to the next slide until it reaches the end.
5 When you reach the end, right click and select 'End Show'.

You are taken back to the original view of your slideshow where you can make any further changes if you need to, or click on the cross to close PowerPoint®.

Summary

In this chapter we have discussed:

- How to use PowerPoint® to create slideshows
- How to select a slide layout
- How to add text, ClipArt and photographs to slides
- How to save the slideshow
- How to run the slideshow

glossary

Chapters where the term is discussed are indicated by the bold numbers at the end of the definition.

address	a way of identifying websites and emails (**10**)
address bar	the place where you type in a web address e.g. www.Hodder.co.uk when using the Internet (**8, 11**)
address book	an option in email software where you can store lists of email addresses (**8**)
adware	bad software that sets itself up on your computer when using the Internet (**16**)
attachment	any file that is sent as well as an email, e.g. a photograph (**9**)
autorun	any CD or DVD will play automatically when put in the computer (**5**)
autosum	a way of adding a formula (calculation) in a spreadsheet (**24**)
backup	a separate copy of your work usually saved onto a CD (**20**)
basket	shows you what you have bought when you are shopping on the Internet (**11**)
blogging	a diary on the Internet (**15**)
bold	a way of making text stand out by making the text darker (**6, 7**)
bookmark	a method of saving an Internet address so that you can go back to the page later; also known as 'Favourites' (**10**)
broadband	high-speed access to the Internet (**1, 13**)

browse	a method of looking through information (**3, 11**)
browser	software for looking at websites (**3, 10**)
browsing	the process of viewing web pages (**12**)
bullet point	a small dot at the beginning of a line of text – used to show a list if items (**7, 27**)
card	a small plastic device inserted into a digital camera that stores the photographs (**2**)
CD-R	a CD that can have information saved to it once (**2, 20**)
CD-RW	a CD that can have information saved to it over and over again (**2, 20**)
cell	one small box in a spreadsheet (**24**)
chat room	a place on a website where you can have online conversations with other people (**13**)
clipart	a library of pictures available in Microsoft® software (**7, 22, 27**)
column	used in spreadsheets to identify a collection of vertical cells; identified by a letter e.g. Column A (**24**)
computer system	the generic term for a combination of the hardware (equipment) and software (programs) (**1**)
copy and paste	a method of taking text or an image in one place and creating a copy of it somewhere else (**7**)
cursor	the small line on the screen that shows you where the text will go when you start typing (**6**)
cut and paste	a method of deleting text or an image from one place and putting it somewhere else (**7**)
database	a collection of information on a related theme (**26**)
data type	in database software, this describes what type of information is being stored, e.g. text or number (**26**)
dead link	a hyperlink from a web page that does not lead to anything (**10**)
desktop	the main way of using Windows software – shows all the icons for the programs and folders on your computer; also, a type of computer that sits on the desk (as opposed to a tower unit) (**1**)

download	the process of getting something from the Internet onto your computer (**3, 5**)
drag	a method of using the mouse where you hold down the left mouse button while moving the mouse (**6, 7, 23**)
DVD-R	a disk that can have information saved to it once (**2, 20**)
DVD-RW	a disk that can have information saved to it over and over again (**2, 20**)
eBay	an online auction site (**12**)
email account	a personal email address (**8**)
email provider	the business that provides you will access to email e.g. Yahoo!, BT, Tiscali, Microsoft (**8**)
field	in database software, this refers to all of the different items of information being stored (**26**)
file	all information stored on the computer is stored in files, so a file could be a document, a slideshow, a photograph or any other kind of information (**4, 6**)
file name	the name given to a file so that you know what it is (**18**)
file type	indicates what type of information is stored in the file, e.g. a document, photographs, etc. (**18**)
file-sharing	websites that allow you to share files (usually music or video) with other people – often illegally (**16**)
Filmstrip view	A way of viewing files in Windows®; particularly useful for looking at photographs (**19**)
filtering or blocking software	software that prevents certain websites from being viewed (**16**)
firewall	a method of stopping hackers getting access to your computer when you are on the Internet (**16**)
flatbed scanner	a device for copying printed documents and turning them into a computerized version (**1, 3, 18**)
floppy disk	a device for storing information (**20**)
folder	a place where files are stored on your computer e.g. My Documents (**4**)
folders tree	a list of all of the folders that are on your computer (**18**)
font	the style of text (**6**)

format	the process of changing the way that something looks on the screen (**6**)
frame	in desktop publishing software, this is a box that has text or pictures in it (**22, 23**)
gigabytes (GB)	a measurement of how much information can be stored on a computer (**1**)
gigahertz (Ghz)	a measurement of the speed of a processor, that is, how fast the computer works (**1**)
hacking	where someone gains unauthorized access to your computer – usually when you are on the Internet (**16**)
hard disk	a device inside the computer where all information is stored (**18**)
hardware	all the physical parts of a computer (**1, 5**)
highlighted	shows when a text or an image has been selected (**6**)
hits	in a search engine, this shows the number of websites that are found when you type in some key words (**10**)
home page	the first page of a website that usually contains an introduction to the website and lots of hyperlinks to other parts of the site (**8**)
hot key	pressing certain combinations of keys as a quicker way of selecting certain options (**6**)
hyperlink	a link from a web page that leads to other web pages (**8, 10**)
icons	small pictures used to represent different things (**4**)
identity theft	when someone pretends to be you with the intention of stealing from you (**16**)
inbox	where messages are stored in email (**8**)
inkjet	a type of printer that uses ink cartridges (**1**)
install	the process of adding new software or hardware to the computer (**5**)
installation routine	the process the computer goes through to add new software (**5**)
Internet	a global connection of computers (**8, 10**)
IP address	the unique number that is assigned to your computer when you are on the Internet (**16**)
iPod™	a device for storing and playing music with headphones (**5**)
iTunes™	software used for downloading and organizing music from the Internet (**5**)

jpg	a file format for photographs and other images (9)
keywords	the main words that you choose to type in when you are searching for something; usually refers to search engines on the Internet (10)
laptop	a portable computer (1)
laser	a type of printer (1)
left-aligned	where text is lined up on the left-hand side (6)
link	*see* hyperlink (8)
load	the process of either installing software, or opening software on your computer (5)
log on	the process of gaining access to a computer, or to websites; usually involves typing in a password (12, 13)
lookup wizard	in databases, a way of creating a drop-down list (26)
mail merge	the process of combining names and address stored in a database, with a standard letter (26)
media player	software for playing music and video (5, 14)
megabytes (MB)	a measurement of how big the computer's memory is (1)
memory stick	a device that plugs into the computer and can be used for storing information (2, 20)
menu	the words across the top of the screen in software that let you get at the various options (4)
minimize	closing a window but leaving it available in the taskbar (4)
modem	a device needed for connecting your computer to the Internet (1, 5)
mouse pointer	the small arrow on the screen that can be controlled by moving the mouse (4, 10)
multimedia	anything that combines text, graphics, sound and video (14)
newsgroup	a way of posting and reading messages on the Internet – organized into topics (13)
numbered point	a way of creating a list with a number in front of each item (7)
online	refers to being on the Internet (5, 11)
online banking	doing your banking on the Internet (15)
operating system	software needed to make your computer work e.g. Windows XP (1)

password	a way of ensuring the correct person is using the computer (**8**, **16**)
PayPal	a method of paying for something that you have bought over the Internet (**12**, **16**)
peripherals	any piece of equipment that can be used in conjunction with your computer e.g. a printer or scanner (**2**)
phishing	where someone tries to get your bank account details from you via email, so that they can steal from you (**16**)
player	*see* media player (**14**)
point size	refers to the size of the font (text) (**6**)
port	a socket on your computer where something can be plugged in (**17**)
portal	a website that provides links to other websites of a similar topic (**15**)
premium dialler	bad software that connects your computer to the Internet at £1.50 or more each minute (**16**)
preview	a way of looking at something on the computer before carrying out an action (**4**, **18**)
print preview	a way of looking at something on the computer before printing (**6**, **7**)
reboot	switching the computer off and on again (**5**)
record	in database software, refers to all the information stored about one person (**26**)
redo	will put back anything that you have just undone using the 'undo' option (**7**)
resolution	the clarity of an image either on screen or printed (**2**, **18**)
restore	making a window bigger or smaller (**4**)
right-aligned	lining up text on the right (**6**)
row	in spreadsheets, refers to each horizontal set of cells (**24**)
scanner	*see* flatbed scanner (**1**)
scroll bar	the method used to move up and down a page (**6**)
scroll down	moving down a page (**8**)
scrolling	the process of moving up, down or across a page (**7**)
search	a method of finding specific information when using the computer (**7**, **11**, **12**, **27**)
search engine	software for searching the Internet (**10**)
secure site	a website that has extra protection for people making online purchases (**10**, **16**)

shortcut	an icon, usually on the desktop that opens a program or folder (**4, 5**)
shut down	the process of switching the computer off (**4**)
slideshow presentation	a way of presenting information to others on the computer (**4, 27**)
software	the programs that run on computers e.g. Windows, Word, etc (**1, 5**)
sort	in databases, or spreadsheets, a method of sequencing information (**27**)
spam	the email equivalent of junk mail (**8**)
spell-checker	automatic checking of spellings (**6**)
spreadsheet	software for handling numerical information (**3, 25**)
spyware	bad software that installs itself on your computer when you are on the Internet (**16**)
start-up routine	the process that your computer goes through when you switch it on (**4**)
storage devices	any device used for storing information e.g. CD, DVD, memory stick (**2**)
subfolder	a folder within a folder; used to store files (**19**)
taskbar	the small bar at the bottom of the screen that shows what programs, folders and files are currently open (**4, 20**)
text wrapping	the way that text will automatically move down to the next line when it runs out of space (**6, 22**)
thread	a topic of discussion in a newsgroup (**13**)
thumbnail	a way of viewing files as a small image – particularly useful for looking through photographs (**9, 17**)
toolbar	a collection of icons in a program; an alternative to using the menus (**4**)
undo	undoes whatever you did last (**7**)
updates	additions to software that provide new features (**3**)
uploading	the process of putting information onto the Internet; can refer to the process of putting information onto your computer, including digital images from a camera (**17**)
USB	a method for connecting devices to your computer (**1, 2**)
USB port	the socket on the front or back of the computer where you plug in a USB device (**1, 2, 20**)

user name/user ID	required for some Internet services along with a password so that you can access them (**12, 16**)
virus	bad software that installs itself on your computer and can cause damage to your computer (**3, 16, 20**)
virus checker	software that prevents viruses damaging your computer (**3, 9**)
VOIP	Voice over Internet Protocol – allows you to make telephone calls over the Internet using your computer (**13**)
web page	a page of information on the Internet (**10**)
web-based	a service that is provided over the Internet (**3, 8**)
website	several pages of information on the Internet (**7, 10**)
Windows® desktop	*see* desktop (**4**)
wizard	a selection of screens that guide you through a particular process (**5, 21**)
WordArt	a way of creating artistic effects with text, available in all Microsoft software (**23**)
word processing	software for typing and creating documents (**6, 7**)
world wide web (www)	the collective name for all the websites and web pages on the Internet (**10**)
worm	*see* virus (**16**)
wrap	*see* text wrapping (**6**)
wrapping	*see* text wrapping (**25**)

index

teach®
yourself

From Advanced Sudoku to Zulu, you'll find everything you need in the **teach yourself** range, in books, on CD and on DVD.

Visit **www.teachyourself.co.uk** for more details.

Advanced Sudoku & Kakuro
Afrikaans
Alexander Technique
Algebra
Ancient Greek
Applied Psychology
Arabic
Aromatherapy
Art History
Astrology
Astronomy
AutoCAD 2004
AutoCAD 2007
Ayurveda
Baby Massage and Yoga
Baby Signing
Baby Sleep
Bach Flower Remedies
Backgammon
Ballroom Dancing
Basic Accounting
Basic Computer Skills
Basic Mathematics
Beauty
Beekeeping
Beginner's Arabic Script
Beginner's Chinese
Beginner's Chinese Script

Beginner's Dutch
Beginner's French
Beginner's German
Beginner's Greek
Beginner's Greek Script
Beginner's Hindi
Beginner's Italian
Beginner's Japanese
Beginner's Japanese Script
Beginner's Latin
Beginner's Portuguese
Beginner's Russian
Beginner's Russian Script
Beginner's Spanish
Beginner's Turkish
Beginner's Urdu Script
Bengali
Better Bridge
Better Chess
Better Driving
Better Handwriting
Biblical Hebrew
Biology
Birdwatching
Blogging
Body Language
Book Keeping
Brazilian Portuguese

Bridge
Buddhism
Bulgarian
Business Chinese
Business French
Business Japanese
Business Plans
Business Spanish
Business Studies
Buying a Home in France
Buying a Home in Italy
Buying a Home in Portugal
Buying a Home in Spain
C++
Calculus
Calligraphy
Cantonese
Car Buying and Maintenance
Card Games
Catalan
Chess
Chi Kung
Chinese Medicine
Chinese
Christianity
Classical Music
Coaching
Collecting
Computing for the Over 50s
Consulting
Copywriting
Correct English
Counselling
Creative Writing
Cricket
Croatian
Crystal Healing
CVs
Czech
Danish
Decluttering
Desktop Publishing
Detox
Digital Photography
Digital Video & PC Editing

Dog Training
Drawing
Dream Interpretation
Dutch
Dutch Conversation
Dutch Dictionary
Dutch Grammar
Eastern Philosophy
Electronics
English as a Foreign Language
English for International
   Business
English Grammar
English Grammar as a Foreign
   Language
English Vocabulary
Entrepreneurship
Estonian
Ethics
Excel 2003
Feng Shui
Film Making
Film Studies
Finance for Non-Financial
   Managers
Finnish
Fitness
Flash 8
Flash MX
Flexible Working
Flirting
Flower Arranging
Franchising
French
French Conversation
French Dictionary
French Grammar
French Phrasebook
French Starter Kit
French Verbs
French Vocabulary
Freud
Gaelic
Gardening
Genetics

Geology
German
German Conversation
German Grammar
German Phrasebook
German Verbs
German Vocabulary
Globalization
Go
Golf
Good Study Skills
Great Sex
Greek
Greek Conversation
Greek Phrasebook
Growing Your Business
Guitar
Gulf Arabic
Hand Reflexology
Hausa
Herbal Medicine
Hieroglyphics
Hindi
Hinduism
Home PC Maintenance and
  Networking
How to DJ
How to Run a Marathon
How to Win at Casino Games
How to Win at Horse Racing
How to Win at Online Gambling
How To Win At Poker
How to Write A Blockbuster
Human Anatomy & Physiology
Hungarian
Icelandic
Improve Your French
Improve Your German
Improve Your Italian
Improve Your Spanish
Improving your Employability
Indian Head Massage
Indonesian
Instant French
Instant German
Instant Greek

Instant Italian
Instant Japanese
Instant Portuguese
Instant Russian
Instant Spanish
Irish
Irish Conversation
Irish Grammar
Islam
Italian
Italian Conversation
Italian Grammar
Italian Phrasebook
Italian Starter Kit
Italian Verbs
Italian Vocabulary
Japanese
Japanese Conversation
Java
JavaScript
Jazz
Jewellery Making
Judaism
Jung
Keeping a Rabbit
Keeping Aquarium Fish
Keeping Pigs
Keeping Poultry
Knitting
Korean
Latin American Spanish
Latin
Latin Dictionary
Latin Grammar
Latvian
Letter Writing Skills
Life at 50: For Men
Life at 50: For Women
Life Coaching
Linguistics
LINUX
Lithuanian
Magic
Mahjong
Malay
Managing Stress

Managing Your Own Career
Mandarin Chinese Conversation
Marketing
Marx
Massage
Mathematics
Meditation
Modern China
Modern Hebrew
Modern Persian
Mosaics
Music Theory
Mussolini's Italy
Nazi Germany
Negotiating
Nepali
New Testament Greek
NLP
Norwegian
Norwegian Conversation
Old English
One-Day French
One-Day French - the DVD
One-Day German
One-Day Greek
One-Day Italian
One-Day Portuguese
One-Day Spanish
One-Day Spanish - the DVD
Origami
Owning a Cat
Owning A Horse
Panjabi
PC Networking for Small
  Businesses
Personal Safety and Self
  Defence
Philosophy
Philosophy of Mind
Philosophy of Religion
Photography
Photoshop
PHP with MySQL
Physics
Piano

Pilates
Planning Your Wedding
Polish
Polish Conversation
Politics
Portuguese
Portuguese Conversation
Portuguese Grammar
Portuguese Phrasebook
Postmodernism
Pottery
PowerPoint 2003
PR
Project Management
Psychology
Quick Fix French Grammar
Quick Fix German Grammar
Quick Fix Italian Grammar
Quick Fix Spanish Grammar
Quick Fix: Access 2002
Quick Fix: Excel 2000
Quick Fix: Excel 2002
Quick Fix: HTML
Quick Fix: Windows XP
Quick Fix: Word
Quilting
Recruitment
Reflexology
Reiki
Relaxation
Retaining Staff
Romanian
Running Your Own Business
Russian
Russian Conversation
Russian Grammar
Sage Line 50
Sanskrit
Screenwriting
Serbian
Setting Up A Small Business
Shorthand Pitman 2000
Sikhism
Singing
Slovene

Small Business Accounting
Small Business Health Check
Songwriting
Spanish
Spanish Conversation
Spanish Dictionary
Spanish Grammar
Spanish Phrasebook
Spanish Starter Kit
Spanish Verbs
Spanish Vocabulary
Speaking On Special Occasions
Speed Reading
Stalin's Russia
Stand Up Comedy
Statistics
Stop Smoking
Sudoku
Swahili
Swahili Dictionary
Swedish
Swedish Conversation
Tagalog
Tai Chi
Tantric Sex
Tap Dancing
Teaching English as a Foreign Language
Teams & Team Working
Thai
The British Empire
The British Monarchy from Henry VIII
The Cold War
The First World War
The History of Ireland
The Internet
The Kama Sutra
The Middle East Since 1945
The Second World War
Theatre
Time Management
Tracing Your Family History
Training
Travel Writing

Trigonometry
Turkish
Turkish Conversation
Twentieth Century USA
Typing
Ukrainian
Understanding Tax for Small Businesses
Understanding Terrorism
Urdu
Vietnamese
Visual Basic
Volcanoes
Watercolour Painting
Weight Control through Diet & Exercise
Welsh
Welsh Dictionary
Welsh Grammar
Wills & Probate
Windows XP
Wine Tasting
Winning at Job Interviews
Word 2003
World Cultures: China
World Cultures: England
World Cultures: Germany
World Cultures: Italy
World Cultures: Japan
World Cultures: Portugal
World Cultures: Russia
World Cultures: Spain
World Cultures: Wales
World Faiths
Writing a Novel
Writing Crime Fiction
Writing for Children
Writing for Magazines
Writing Poetry
Xhosa
Yiddish
Yoga
Zen
Zulu